Solzhenitsyn at Harvard

Solzhenitsyn at Harvard

*The Address,
Twelve Early Responses,
and Six Later Reflections*

Ronald Berman   Richard Pipes
Sidney Hook   William H. McNeill
Harold J. Berman   Michael Novak

Edited by Ronald Berman

Ethics and Public Policy Center
Washington, D.C.

THE ETHICS AND PUBLIC POLICY CENTER, established in 1976, conducts a program of research, writing, publications, and conferences to encourage debate on domestic and foreign policy issues among religious, educational, academic, business, political, and other leaders. A nonpartisan effort, the Center is supported by contributions from foundations, corporations, and individuals. The authors alone are responsible for the views expressed in Center publications.

Library of Congress Cataloging in Publication Data:
Main entry under title:
Solzhenitsyn at Harvard.
   1. Solzhenitsyn, Aleksandr Isaevich, 1918–
Raskolotyi mir—Addresses, essays, lectures. 2. Civilization, Occidental—Addresses, essays, lectures.
3. Civilization, Modern—1950–   —Addresses, essays,
lectures. 4. Communism—Addresses, essays, lectures.
5. Europe, Eastern—Civilization—Addresses, essays,
lectures. I. Berman, Ronald. II. Solzhenitsyn,
Aleksandr Isaevich, 1918–   Raskolotyi mir. English.
1979.
CB245.S5693S64   909.82   79-26033
ISBN 0-89633-034-6
ISBN 0-89633-023-0 pbk.

$9.50 cloth, $5.00 paper

Contents

Foreword

ALEKSANDR SOLZHENITSYN HAS MADE a scathing indictment of the Soviet totalitarian system in his monumental *Gulag Archipelago*. During the days of Stalin the Soviet state was "girded with hoops of steel," he said in the third volume, written in 1968. "The hoops are still there. There is no law. . . . The same treacherous secrecy, the same fog of injustice, still hangs in our air."

A decade later Solzhenitsyn turned his formidable powers of critical analysis to the West and found it wanting. By any measure his speech at Harvard University in June 1978 was a historic statement, and it was so treated by the American press. But much of the comment in the media was confused and superficial. This study is a modest effort to place Solzhenitsyn's ideas in historical, political, and philosophical perspective.

The Harvard address as published by Harper & Row makes up the first part of this book. The address is followed by a representative selection of early newspaper and journal comment on it. The last part of the volume includes new essays from six vantage points: Richard Pipes is a Russian specialist, Michael Novak a theologian, William H. McNeill an expert in world history, Sidney Hook a philosopher, Harold J. Berman an expert in law, and Ronald Berman a literary scholar.

Professor Ronald Berman is the editor of the volume as well as the author of one of its essays. Formerly chairman of the National

Endowment for the Humanities, he now teaches literature at the University of California at San Diego. I am grateful to him for his double contribution. I also wish to express appreciation to the publishers of articles that appeared elsewhere for their kind permission to include them here.

The publication of this book was delayed for many months by Solzhenitsyn's refusal—communicated through the publisher of the Harvard address, Harper & Row—to allow us to reprint the speech. His persistently adamant stand was very puzzling to us; the text had previously been printed in several newspapers and magazines, and our book was clearly a serious effort to present his views and thoughtful comments on them to a wider audience. Thinking that we were forbidden to use only the published version of the address, we then had a new translation made by Professor Helen Yakobson of George Washington University. This process of seeking permission and producing a new translation consumed the better part of a year.

Finally, in January 1980, the book was ready to go to press. We sent page proofs to Solzhenitsyn and invited him and his wife to come to Washington at our expense to attend a press lunch launching the book. The reply was a phone call and a follow-up telegram from Harper & Row asserting that our publication of the address in any translation would be considered a violation of the author's copyright rights and theirs. We then tried, both directly (no easy task with someone who has isolated himself in rural Vermont) and through intermediaries, to get Solzhenitsyn to relent. He would not.

On April 30 of this year a legal complaint was filed on our behalf in the U.S. District Court for the District of Columbia, asking that Solzhenitsyn and Harper & Row be prohibited from charging us with copyright infringement if we published the address in our book. The complaint alleged that the threats of copyright infringement against us violated our First Amendment rights and the "fair use" provisions of the copyright law. A week later Harper & Row notified our lawyers that we had been granted permission to reprint the Harper & Row version of the speech. Our complaint was withdrawn, and we found ourselves standing firmly on the ground we had thought we were on fourteen months before.

We are greatly indebted to our lawyers, Donald A. Kaul, Peter J. Klarfeld, and Robert A. Smith, of the Washington firm of Brownstein, Zeidman and Schomer. They were friendly, enthusiastic, thorough, and efficient—as well as effective. And they worked without cost to us, under the *pro bono* guidelines of their firm.

In Part Three of this book, the quotations from the speech conform to the new translation we had prepared, which varies slightly in style but not in substance from the copyrighted translation printed in Part One.

This volume published by the Ethics and Public Policy Center is one of a series of studies dealing with central political and moral issues of our time. Earlier studies include *Decline of the West? George Kennan and His Critics, Morality and Foreign Policy: A Symposium on President Carter's Stance,* and *The CIA and the American Ethic.* The views expressed in all Center publications are those of the authors.

ERNEST W. LEFEVER, *President*
Ethics and Public Policy Center

Washington, D.C.
May 1980

Introduction

RONALD BERMAN

COMMENCEMENT ADDRESSES SELDOM make news, but the speech given at Harvard University in June 1978 may become the best known since Winston Churchill told an audience in Fulton, Missouri, that an Iron Curtain had descended across the European continent. The Harvard speech was given in Russian by Aleksandr Solzhenitsyn and translated to an audience and, later, a society unprepared for his opinions. The speech set off an avalanche of critical misunderstanding.

This book contains the address, entitled "A World Split Apart," a spectrum of early responses to it, and essays by specialists on major themes it suggests. The translated text, like the Russian original, is divided into seventeen parts with subheadings. These seventeen parts may be grouped into six units, each developing a particular line of thought.

The first unit describes the present world situation. Instead of the "one world" that we have mistakenly desired, there are opposing worlds: those of the United States, the Soviet Union, and other nations. The West is much mistaken in believing that international politics will imitate the ideas and forms of democracy; it deludes itself by the theory of convergence. As Solzhenitsyn sees it, the world is split among powers that are fundamentally different and permanently hostile.

In the second unit Solzhenitsyn describes the West as he sees it today. The West has little will to assert itself, he says. It has become materialistic and has forgotten the ideals that first generated its growth and excellence. Freedom has now become indifference, attentive only to private desires.

The third unit centers on the abuses of the press in a democracy and on the confused role of intellectuals. It argues that democratic public opinion is badly misinformed.

In the fourth unit Solzhenitsyn expresses his opposition to *both* democracy and socialism.

The fifth unit takes up the West's duty—often neglected—to preserve freedom. It argues that the West will never prevail against Communism unless it is prepared to make great sacrifices.

The last unit begins with an analysis of humanism, which the author believes has declined into the worship of man and his works. A summary of Solzhenitsyn's judgment of the West was implied by Emerson's reaction to the world of industrialism, that "Things are in the saddle,/and ride mankind." Solzhenitsyn argues that Communism and democracy derive from the same roots in the secular Enlightenment, and that because of this, Western intellectuals hesitate to criticize the effects of Communism. He concludes that we are now at a moment of decision: we must choose either to sink completely into materialism or to pursue a freedom grounded in spiritual values.

Major American newspapers gave wide coverage to the Harvard speech and took up its points in columns and editorials. The *New York Times* and the *Washington Post* asserted that Solzhenitsyn did not really understand the United States. Coming from the most tightly organized of all despotisms, he was said to be incapable of seeing in freedom anything more than anarchy. His religious values and his politics were judged to be dangerous because they leave no room for maneuver between Communism and democracy. He was numbered among those who would prolong the Cold War. And it was suggested that he was something of a fanatic.

In general, conservatives seemed more sympathetic to the speech than liberals. *National Review* noted in an essay and an editorial that "A World Split Apart" had the discomforting virtue of accuracy; its diagnosis of the world situation, of Soviet intentions, and of American foreign policy seemed essentially correct. Much less credence was given to Solzhenitsyn's knowledge of American society. Among the points raised by the columnist George Will were that Solzhenitsyn's moral concerns seem unfamiliar to a society embodying liberal relativism, and that he stands in a long line of philosophers, from Cicero through Pascal, who have made a good deal of sense interpreting the world from religious and moral perspectives.

The essay by Olga Andreyev Carlisle directs us to the history of Russian nationalism. Mrs. Carlisle, who has known Solzhenitsyn and been involved in his *samizdat* publication, believes that the speech emphasizes the values of the Russian Orthodox Church. The point is elaborated by Jack Fruchtman, Jr., who perceives Solzhenitsyn as a twentieth-century Slavophile, that is, a Russian intellectual who defines his beliefs by hostility to Western materialism, faith in Russian identity and destiny, and religious orthodoxy.

Arthur Schlesinger, Jr., provides the most extensive of the early responses. He begins by pointing out that the Puritans who founded Harvard might well have found themselves a good deal closer to Solzhenitsyn than to their own descendants. Schlesinger suggests that there is an opposition of religious or absolute truth to secular or relative truth. Like the Puritans, he says, Solzhenitsyn has no particular use for freedom, and little for democracy. While giving Solzhenitsyn ample credit for his moral vision and his critique of Communism, Schlesinger states that there are limits to prophetic vision: though equipped with an imagination denied his critics, Solzhenitsyn does not provide either an accurate picture of America or workable ideas for its politics.

On the debit side, Solzhenitsyn was seen by these early commentators to be an obstacle to the ending of the Cold War, to be unduly influenced by religion, to misunderstand democracy, and to love us insufficiently. Rosalynn Carter, the First Lady, defended the goodness of American society at a press conference. There followed a great many journalistic apologies for the nation and for the media that Solzhenitsyn had so resoundingly attacked. On the credit side, he was said to have recognized the nature of our enemy, called us to a much needed accounting for our materialism, inspired us to transcend ourselves, and set a great personal example of courage. For the most part the media conveyed the possibility of sympathizing with his feelings but not with his ideas.

Six new interpretative essays make up Part Three of this book. Richard Pipes of Harvard University covers Russian intellectual and political history; Michael Novak of the American Enterprise Institute deals with Solzhenitsyn's theology; William H. McNeill of the University of Chicago considers the role of the West in world history; Harold J. Berman of the Harvard Law School analyzes Solzhenitsyn's conception of Western law; Sidney Hook criticizes the speech from the viewpoint of philosophy; and I have undertaken to suggest Solzhenitsyn's relation to other modern writers.

In examining the tradition within which Solzhenitsyn writes, Pipes emphasizes those nineteenth-century conservative ideas that impelled the Slavophile movement. Pipes observes that these ideas come to us through the novels of Dostoevsky as well as through the politics of Russian nationalism. He views Solzhenitsyn as something of a twentieth-century Slavophile, continuing the battle against the empty and formalistic institutions of the West.

Michael Novak points out that Solzhenitsyn embraces a familiar and traditional Catholic critique of secular humanism. In that tradition it is usual to assert that after the Renaissance the nations of the West gave up the worship of God and began to worship Man. The great advantage of this critique of humanism is that it escapes excessive optimism. Solzhenitsyn, like other religious philosophers, finds in Christian thought an understanding of human character more accurate than that provided by any secular mythology. A good deal of the criticism of "A World Split Apart" assumes that the authority of the speech was weakened by a religious view of human nature. Novak suggests that, on the contrary, Solzhenitsyn's religious world view is the chief source of his moral, psychological, and political insight.

William McNeill examines the Harvard address from another

point of view, that of a world historian. He concludes that few
tactics are available to the United States for pursuing the conflict
with Communism. But he is a good deal more favorably impressed than Solzhenitsyn with the staying power of the West and
with its secular virtues. In his view there has not been a basic
failure of will, although we in the West have trouble dealing with
our deficiencies.

Harold J. Berman traces Solzhenitsyn's attack on Western
"legalism" to the traditional Russian Orthodox emphasis on spirituality and sacrifice in contrast to law, which is thought to be hard,
cold, impersonal, and rationalistic. In the West, on the contrary,
law has traditionally been viewed in part as "a way of translating
both justice and love into social situations involving large numbers
of people." Berman concludes that a new integration of the positive values of both East and West is needed if mankind is to enter
the new stage to which Solzhenitsyn calls us.

Sidney Hook writes of four main points of contention. He
agrees with Solzhenitsyn that freedom cannot be unqualified. He
also agrees that in the name of absolute freedom the West has
become obsessed with its own well-being. As Hook sees it, we are
in fact legalistic—though Solzhenitsyn has an incomplete and in
some respects erroneous conception of American law. As for the
press, Hook suggests that Solzhenitsyn concentrates on the
wrong point: the press abuses its privilege and its power, but a
free press is one of the risks we undertake in order to have a
functioning democracy. Finally, Hook resists the notion that
morality is a product only of religious belief; he writes from the
point of view of a philosopher who perceives political morality to
be both desirable and attainable without the intervention of religious institutions or belief. His conclusion is that Solzhenitsyn's
powerful sense of Western history and destiny matters far more
than the errors he has made in interpreting our style and condition.

My own essay suggests that Aleksandr Solzhenitsyn is not so
strange to us as he may first appear. He says about the West what
has often been said in satire—and what in our time has been the

burden of many poets, novelists, and artists. It is a common theme of modern criticism that our society has failed us; and novelists like Conrad, poets like Pound, and philosophers like T. E. Hulme have given us rather a lot of chapter and verse on the subject. When Solzhenitsyn attacks the materialism we display, he is sharing the attitudes of a good many other winners of the Nobel Prize.

PART ONE

THE ADDRESS

ALEKSANDR I. SOLZHENITSYN

A World Split Apart

I am sincerely happy to be here with you on the occasion of the 327th commencement of this old and illustrious university. My congratulations and best wishes to all of today's graduates.

Harvard's motto is "Veritas." Many of you have already found out and others will find out in the course of their lives that truth eludes us as soon as our concentration begins to flag, all the while leaving the illusion that we are continuing to pursue it. This is the source of much discord. Also, truth seldom is sweet; it is almost invariably bitter. A measure of bitter truth is included in my speech today, but I offer it as a friend, not as an adversary.

Three years ago in the United States I said certain things that were rejected and appeared unacceptable. Today, however, many people agree with what I then said. . . .

The split in today's world is perceptible even to a hasty glance. Any of our contemporaries readily identifies two world powers, each of them already capable of utterly destroying the other. However, the understanding of the split too often is limited to this political conception: the illusion according to which danger may be abolished through successful diplomatic negotiations or by achieving a balance of armed forces. The truth is that the split is · both more profound and more alienating, that the rifts are more numerous than one can see at first glance. The deep manifold splits bear the danger of equally manifold disaster for all of us, in accordance with the ancient truth that a kingdom—in this case, our Earth—divided against itself cannot stand.

3

Contemporary Worlds

There is the concept of the Third World: thus, we already have three worlds. Undoubtedly, however, the number is even greater; we are just too far away to see. Every ancient and deeply rooted self-contained culture, especially if it is spread over a wide part of the earth's surface, constitutes a self-contained world, full of riddles and surprises to Western thinking. As a minimum, we must include in this category China, India, the Muslim world, and Africa, if indeed we accept the approximation of viewing the latter two as uniform. For one thousand years Russia belonged to such a category, although Western thinking systematically committed the mistake of denying its special character and therefore never understood it, just as today the West does not understand Russia in Communist captivity. And while it may be that in past years Japan has increasingly become, in effect, a Far West, drawing ever closer to Western ways (I am no judge here), Israel, I think, should not be reckoned as part of the West, if only because of the decisive circumstance that its state system is fundamentally linked to religion.

How short a time ago, relatively, the small world of modern Europe was easily seizing colonies all over the globe, not only without anticipating any real resistance, but usually with contempt for any possible values in the conquered peoples' approach to life. It all seemed an overwhelming success, with no geographic limits. Western society expanded in a triumph of human independence and power. And all of a sudden the twentieth century brought the clear realization of this society's fragility. We now see that the conquests proved to be short-lived and precarious (and this, in turn, points to defects in the Western view of the world which led to these conquests). Relations with the former colonial world now have switched to the opposite extreme and the Western world often exhibits an excess of obsequiousness, but it is difficult yet to estimate the size of the bill which former colonial countries will present to the West and it is difficult to predict whether the surrender not only of its last colonies, but of everything it owns, will be sufficient for the West to clear this account.

Convergence

But the persisting blindness of superiority continues to hold the belief that all the vast regions of our planet should develop and mature to the level of contemporary Western systems, the best in theory and the most attractive in practice; that all those other worlds are but temporarily prevented (by wicked leaders or by severe crises or by their own barbarity and incomprehension) from pursuing Western pluralistic democracy and adopting the Western way of life. Countries are judged on the merit of their ' progress in that direction. But in fact such a conception is a fruit of Western incomprehension of the essence of other worlds, a result of mistakenly measuring them all with a Western yardstick. The real picture of our planet's development bears little resemblance to all this.

The anguish of a divided world gave birth to the theory of ' convergence between the leading Western countries and the Soviet Union. It is a soothing theory which overlooks the fact that these worlds are not at all evolving toward each other and that neither one can be transformed into the other without violence. ' Besides, convergence inevitably means acceptance of the other side's defects, too, and this can hardly suit anyone.

If I were today addressing an audience in my country, in my examination of the overall pattern of the world's rifts I would have concentrated on the calamities of the East. But since my forced exile in the West has now lasted four years and since my audience is a Western one, I think it may be of greater interest to concentrate on certain aspects of the contemporary West, such as I see them.

A Decline in Courage

A decline in courage may be the most striking feature that an ' outside observer notices in the West today. The Western world has lost its civic courage, both as a whole and separately, in each country, in each government, in each political party, and of course, in the United Nations. Such a decline in courage is par-

ticularly noticeable among the ruling and intellectual elites, caus-
ing an impression of a loss of courage by the entire society. There
remain many courageous individuals, but they have no determin-
ing influence on public life. Political and intellectual functionaries
exhibit this depression, passivity, and perplexity in their actions
and in their statements, and even more so in their self-serving
rationales as to how realistic, reasonable, and intellectually and
even morally justified it is to base state policies on weakness and
cowardice. And the decline in courage, at times attaining what
could be termed a lack of manhood, is ironically emphasized by
occasional outbursts of boldness and inflexibility on the part of
those same functionaries when dealing with weak governments
and with countries that lack support, or with doomed currents
which clearly cannot offer any resistance. But they get tongue-
tied and paralyzed when they deal with powerful governments
and threatening forces, with aggressors and international terrorists.

Must one point out that from ancient times a decline in courage
has been considered the first symptom of the end?

Well-Being

When the modern Western states were being formed, it was
proclaimed as a principle that governments are meant to serve
man and that man lives in order to be free and pursue happiness.
(See, for example, the American Declaration of Independence.)
Now at last during past decades technical and social progress has
permitted the realization of such aspirations: the welfare state.
Every citizen has been granted the desired freedom and material
goods in such quantity and of such quality as to guarantee in
theory the achievement of happiness, in the debased sense of the
word which has come into being during those same decades. (In
the process, however, one psychological detail has been over-
looked: the constant desire to have still more things and a still
better life and the struggle to this end imprint many Western faces
with worry and even depression, though it is customary to carefully conceal such feelings. This active and tense competition
comes to dominate all human thought and does not in the least

open a way to free spiritual development.) The individual's independence from many types of state pressure has been guaranteed; the majority of the people have been granted well-being to an extent their fathers and grandfathers could not even dream about; it has become possible to raise young people according to these ideals, preparing them for and summoning them toward physical bloom, happiness, the possession of material goods, money, and leisure, toward an almost unlimited freedom in the choice of pleasures. So who should now renounce all this, why and for the sake of what should one risk one's precious life in defense of the common good and particularly in the nebulous case when the security of one's nation must be defended in an as yet distant land?

Even biology tells us that a high degree of habitual well-being is not advantageous to a living organism. Today, well-being in the life of Western society has begun to take off its pernicious mask.

Legalistic Life

Western society has chosen for itself the organization best suited to its purposes and one I might call legalistic. The limits of human rights and rightness are determined by a system of laws; such limits are very broad. People in the West have acquired considerable skill in using, interpreting, and manipulating law (though laws tend to be too complicated for an average person to understand without the help of an expert). Every conflict is solved according to the letter of the law and this is considered to be the ultimate solution. If one is right from a legal point of view, nothing more is required, nobody may mention that one could still not be entirely right, and urge self-restraint or a renunciation of these rights, call for sacrifice and selfless risk: this would simply sound absurd. Voluntary self-restraint is almost unheard of: everybody strives toward further expansion to the extreme limit of the legal frames. (An oil company is legally blameless when it buys up an invention of a new type of energy in order to prevent its use. A food product manufacturer is legally blameless when he poisons his produce to make it last longer: after all, people are free not to purchase it.)

I have spent all my life under a Communist regime and I will tell you that a society without any objective legal scale is a terrible one indeed. But a society with no other scale but the legal one is also less than worthy of man. A society based on the letter of the law and never reaching any higher fails to take advantage of the full range of human possibilities. The letter of the law is too cold and formal to have a beneficial influence on society. Whenever the tissue of life is woven of legalistic relationships, this creates an atmosphere of spiritual mediocrity that paralyzes man's noblest impulses.

And it will be simply impossible to bear up to the trials of this threatening century with nothing but the supports of a legalistic structure.

The Direction of Freedom

Today's Western society has revealed the inequality between the freedom for good deeds and the freedom for evil deeds. A statesman who wants to achieve something important and highly constructive for his country has to move cautiously and even timidly; thousands of hasty (and irresponsible) critics cling to him at all times; he is constantly rebuffed by parliament and the press. He has to prove that his every step is well-founded and absolutely flawless. Indeed, an outstanding, truly great person who has unusual and unexpected initiatives in mind does not get any chance to assert himself; dozens of traps will be set for him from the beginning. Thus mediocrity triumphs under the guise of democratic restraints.

It is feasible and easy everywhere to undermine administrative power and it has in fact been drastically weakened in all Western countries. The defense of individual rights has reached such extremes as to make society as a whole defenseless against certain individuals. It is time, in the West, to defend not so much human rights as human obligations.

On the other hand, destructive and irresponsible freedom has been granted boundless space. Society has turned out to have scarce defense against the abyss of human decadence, for example against the misuse of liberty for moral violence against young people, such as motion pictures full of pornography, crime, and horror. This is all considered to be part of freedom and to be counterbalanced, in theory, by the young people's right not to look and not to accept. Life organized legalistically has thus shown its inability to defend itself against the corrosion of evil.

And what shall we say about the dark realms of overt criminality? Legal limits (especially in the United States) are broad enough to encourage not only individual freedom but also some misuse of such freedom. The culprit can go unpunished or obtain undeserved leniency—all with the support of thousands of defenders in the society. When a government earnestly undertakes to root out terrorism, public opinion immediately accuses it of violating the terrorists' civil rights. There is quite a number of such cases.

This tilt of freedom toward evil has come about gradually, but it evidently stems from a humanistic and benevolent concept according to which man—the master of this world—does not bear any evil within himself, and all the defects of life are caused by misguided social systems, which must therefore be corrected. Yet strangely enough, though the best social conditions have been achieved in the West, there still remains a great deal of crime; there even is considerably more of it than in the destitute and lawless Soviety society. (There is a multitude of prisoners in our camps who are termed criminals, but most of them never committed any crime; they merely tried to defend themselves against a lawless state by resorting to means outside the legal framework.)

The Direction of the Press

The press, too, of course, enjoys the widest freedom. (I shall be using the word "press" to include all the media.) But what use does it make of it?

Here again, the overriding concern is not to infringe the letter of the law. There is no true moral responsibility for distortion or disproportion. What sort of responsibility does a journalist or a newspaper have to the readership or to history? If they have misled public opinion by inaccurate information or wrong conclusions, even if they have contributed to mistakes on a state level, do we know of any case of open regret voiced by the same journalist or the same newspaper? No; this would damage sales. A nation may be the worse for such a mistake, but the journalist always gets away with it. It is most likely that he will start writing the exact opposite to his previous statements with renewed aplomb.

Because instant and credible information is required, it becomes necessary to resort to guesswork, rumors, and suppositions to fill in the voids, and none of them will ever be refuted; they settle into the readers' memory. How many hasty, immature, superficial, and misleading judgments are expressed every day, confusing readers, and are then left hanging? The press can act the role of public opinion or miseducate it. Thus we may see terrorists heroized, or secret matters pertaining to the nation's defense publicly revealed, or we may witness shameless intrusion into the privacy of well-known people according to the slogan "Everyone is entitled to know everything." (But this is a false slogan of a false era; far greater in value is the forfeited right of people *not to know,* not to have their divine souls stuffed with gossip, nonsense, vain talk. A person who works and leads a meaningful life has no need for this excessive and burdening flow of information.)

Hastiness and superficiality—these are the psychic diseases of the twentieth century and more than anywhere else this is manifested in the press. In-depth analysis of a problem is anathema to the press; it is contrary to its nature. The press merely picks out sensational formulas.

Such as it is, however, the press has become the greatest power within the Western countries, exceeding that of the legislature, the executive, and the judiciary. Yet one would like to ask: According to what law has it been elected and to whom is it responsible? In the Communist East, a journalist is frankly appointed as a state official. But who has voted Western journalists into their positions of power, for how long, and with what prerogatives?

There is yet another surprise for someone coming from the totalitarian East with its rigorously unified press: One discovers a common trend of preferences within the Western press as a whole (the spirit of the time), generally accepted patterns of judgment, and maybe common corporate interests, the sum effect being not competition but unification. Unrestrained freedom exists for the press, but not for the readership, because newspapers mostly transmit in a forceful and emphatic way those opinions which do not too openly contradict their own and that general trend.

A Fashion in Thinking

Without any censorship in the West, fashionable trends of thought and ideas are fastidiously separated from those that are not fashionable, and the latter, without ever being forbidden, have little chance of finding their way into periodicals or books or being heard in colleges. Your scholars are free in the legal sense, but they are hemmed in by the idols of the prevailing fad. There is no open violence, as in the East; however, a selection dictated by fashion and the need to accommodate mass standards frequently prevents the most independent-minded persons from contributing to public life and gives rise to dangerous herd instincts that block successful development. In America, I have received letters from highly intelligent persons—maybe a teacher in a faraway small college who could do much for the renewal and salvation of his country, but the country cannot hear him because the media will not provide him with a forum. This gives birth to strong mass prejudices, to a blindness which is perilous in our dynamic era. An example is the self-deluding interpretation of the state of affairs in the contemporary world that functions as a sort of a petrified armor around people's minds, to such a degree that human voices from seventeen countries of Eastern Europe and Eastern Asia cannot pierce it. It will be broken only by the inexorable crowbar of events.

I have mentioned a few traits of Western life which surprise and shock a new arrival to this world. The purpose and scope of this speech will not allow me to continue such a survey, in particular to look into the impact of these characteristics on important aspects of a nation's life, such as elementary education, advanced education in the humanities, and art.

Socialism

It is almost universally recognized that the West shows all the world the way to successful economic development, even though in past years it has been sharply offset by chaotic inflation. However, many people living in the West are dissatisfied with their own society. They despise it or accuse it of no longer being up to the level of maturity attained by mankind. And this causes many to sway toward socialism, which is a false and dangerous current.

I hope that no one present will suspect me of expressing my partial criticism of the Western system in order to suggest socialism as an alternative. No; with the experience of a country where socialism has been realized, I shall certainly not speak for such an alternative. The mathematician Igor Shafarevich, a member of the Soviet Academy of Science, has written a brilliantly argued book entitled *Socialism;* this is a penetrating historical analysis demonstrating that socialism of any type and shade leads to a total destruction of the human spirit and to a leveling of mankind into death. Shafarevich's book was published in France almost two years ago and so far no one has been found to refute it. It will shortly be published in English in the United States.

Not a Model

But should I be asked, instead, whether I would propose the West, such as it is today, as a model to my country, I would frankly have to answer negatively. No, I could not recommend your society as an ideal for the transformation of ours. Through deep suffering, people in our country have now achieved a spiritual development of such intensity that the Western system in its present state of spiritual exhaustion does not look attractive. Even those characteristics of your life which I have just enumerated are extremely saddening.

A fact which cannot be disputed is the weakening of human personality in the West while in the East it has become firmer and stronger. Six decades for our people and three decades for the people of Eastern Europe; during that time we have been through a spiritual training far in advance of Western experience. The complex and deadly crush of life has produced stronger, deeper, and more interesting personalities than those generated by stand- ardized Western well-being. Therefore, if our society were to be transformed into yours, it would mean an improvement in certain aspects, but also a change for the worse on some particularly significant points. Of course, a society cannot remain in an abyss of lawlessness, as is the case in our country. But it is also demean- ing for it to stay on such a soulless and smooth plane of legalism, as is the case in yours. After the suffering of decades of violence and oppression, the human soul longs for things higher, warmer, and purer than those offered by today's mass living habits, intro- duced as by a calling card by the revolting invasion of commercial advertising, by TV stupor, and by intolerable music.

All this is visible to numerous observers from all the worlds of our planet. The Western way of life is less and less likely to become the leading model.

There are telltale symptoms by which history gives warning to a threatened or perishing society. Such are, for instance, a decline of the arts or a lack of great statesmen. Indeed, sometimes the warnings are quite explicit and concrete. The center of your de- mocracy and of your culture is left without electric power for a few hours only, and all of a sudden crowds of American citizens start looting and creating havoc. The smooth surface film must be very thin, then, the social system quite unstable and unhealthy.

But the fight for our planet, physical and spiritual, a fight of cosmic proportions, is not a vague matter of the future; it has already started. The forces of Evil have begun their decisive of- fensive. You can feel their pressure, yet your screens and publica- tions are full of prescribed smiles and raised glasses. What is the joy about?

Short-sightedness

Very well known representatives of your society, such as George Kennan, say: "We cannot apply moral criteria to poli- tics." Thus we mix good and evil, right and wrong, and make space for the absolute triumph of absolute evil in the world. Only moral criteria can help the West against communism's well-planned world strategy. There are no other criteria. Practical or occasional considerations of any kind will inevitably be swept away by strategy. After a certain level of the problem has been reached, legalistic thinking induces paralysis; it prevents one from seeing the scale and the meaning of events.

In spite of the abundance of information, or maybe partly because of it, the West has great difficulty in finding its bearings amid contemporary events. There have been naïve predictions by some American experts who believed that Angola would become the Soviet Union's Vietnam or that the impudent Cuban expeditions in Africa would best be stopped by special U.S. courtesy to Cuba. Kennan's advice to his own country—to begin unilateral disarmament—belongs to the same category. If you only knew how the youngest of the officials in Moscow's Old Square* roar with laughter at your political wizards! As to Fidel Castro, he openly scorns the United States, boldly sending his troops to distant adventures from his country right next to yours.

However, the most cruel mistake occurred with the failure to understand the Vietnam war. Some people sincerely wanted all wars to stop just as soon as possible; others believed that the way should be left open for national, or Communist, self-determination in Vietnam (or in Cambodia, as we see today with particular clarity). But in fact, members of the U.S. antiwar movement became accomplices in the betrayal of Far Eastern nations, in the genocide and the suffering today imposed on thirty million people there. Do these convinced pacifists now hear the moans coming from there? Do they understand their responsibility today? Or do they prefer not to hear? The American intelligentsia lost its nerve and as a consequence the danger has come much closer to the United States. But there is no awareness of this. Your short-sighted politician who signed the hasty Vietnam capitulation seemingly gave America a carefree breathing pause; however, a hundredfold Vietnam now looms over you. Small Vietnam had been a warning and an occasion to mobilize the nation's courage. But if the full might of America suffered a full-

---

*The Old Square in Moscow *(Staraya Ploshchad)* is the place where the headquarters of the Central Committee of the CPSU are located; it is the real name of what in the West is conventionally referred to as the Kremlin.

fledged defeat at the hands of a small Communist half-country, how can the West hope to stand firm in the future?

I have said on another occasion that in the twentieth century Western democracy has not won any major war by itself; each time it shielded itself with an ally possessing a powerful land army, whose philosophy it did not question. In World War II against Hitler, instead of winning the conflict with its own forces, which would certanly have been sufficient, Western democracy raised up another enemy, one that would prove worse and more powerful, since Hitler had neither the resources nor the people, nor the ideas with broad appeal, nor such a large number of supporters in the West—a fifth column—as the Soviet Union possessed. Some Western voices already have spoken of the need of a protective screen against hostile forces in the next world conflict; in this case, the shield would be China. But I would not wish such an outcome to any country in the world. First of all, it is again a doomed alliance with evil; it would grant the United States a respite, but when at a later date China with its billion people would turn around armed with American weapons, America itself would fall victim to a Cambodia-style genocide.

Loss of Will

And yet, no weapons, no matter how powerful, can help the West until it overcomes its loss of will power. In a state of psychological weakness, weapons even become a burden for the capitulating side. To defend oneself, one must also be ready to die; there is little such readiness in a society raised in the cult of material well-being. Nothing is left, in this case, but concessions, attempts to gain time, and betrayal. Thus at the shameful Belgrade conference, free Western diplomats in their weakness surrendered the line of defense for which enslaved members of the Helsinki Watch Groups are sacrificing their lives.

Western thinking has become conservative: the world situation must stay as it is at any cost; there must be no changes. This debilitating dream of a status quo is the symptom of a society that has ceased to develop. But one must be blind in order not to see that the oceans no longer belong to the West, while the land under its domination keeps shrinking. The two so-called world wars (they were by far not on a world scale, not yet) constituted the internal self-destruction of the small progressive West which has thus prepared its own end. The next war (which does not have to be an atomic one; I do not believe it will be) may well bury Western civilization forever.

In the face of such danger, with such historical values in your past, with such a high level of attained freedom and, apparently, a devotion to it, how is it possible to lose to such an extent the will to defend oneself?

Humanism and Its Consequences

How has this unfavorable relation of forces come about? How did the West decline from its triumphal march to its present debility? Have there been fatal turns and losses of direction in its development? It does not seem so. The West kept advancing steadily in accordance with its proclaimed social intentions, hand in hand with a dazzling progress in technology. And all of a sudden it found itself in its present state of weakness.

This means that the mistake must be at the root, at the very foundation of thought in modern times. I refer to the prevailing Western view of the world which was born in the Renaissance and has found political expression since the Age of Enlightenment. It became the basis for political and social doctrine and could be called rationalistic humanism or humanistic autonomy: the proclaimed and practiced autonomy of man from any higher force above him. It could also be called anthropocentricity, with man seen as the center of all.

The turn introduced by the Renaissance was probably inevitable historically: the Middle Ages had come to a natural end by exhaustion, having become an intolerable despotic repression of man's physical nature in favor of the spiritual one. But then we recoiled from the spirit and embraced all that is material, excessively and incommensurately. The humanistic way of thinking, which has proclaimed itself our guide, did not admit the existence of intrinsic evil in man, nor did it see any task higher than the attainment of happiness on earth. It started modern Western

civilization on the dangerous trend of worshiping man and his
material needs. Everything beyond physical well-being and the
accumulation of material goods, all other human requirements
and characteristics of a subtler and higher nature, were left outside the area of attention of state and social systems, as if human
life did not have any higher meaning. Thus gaps were left open for
evil, and its drafts blow freely today. Mere freedom per se does
not in the least solve all the problems of human life and even adds
a number of new ones.

And yet in early democracies, as in American democracy at the
time of its birth, all individual human rights were granted on the
ground that man is God's creature. That is, freedom was given to
the individual conditionally, in the assumption of his constant
religious responsibility. Such was the heritage of the preceding
one thousand years. Two hundred or even fifty years ago, it would
have seemed quite impossible, in America, that an individual be
granted boundless freedom with no purpose, simply for the satis-
faction of his whims. Subsequently, however, all such limitations
were eroded everywhere in the West; a total emancipation occurred from the moral heritage of Christian centuries with their
great reserves of mercy and sacrifice. State systems were becoming ever more materialistic. The West has finally achieved the
rights of man, and even to excess, but man's sense of responsibility to God and society has grown dimmer and dimmer. In the past
decades, the legalistic selfishness of the Western approach to the
world has reached its peak and the world has found itself in a
harsh spiritual crisis and a political impasse. All the celebrated
technological achievements of progress, including the conquest of
outer space, do not redeem the twentieth century's moral poverty, which no one could have imagined even as late as the
nineteenth century.

An Unexpected Kinship

As humanism in its development was becoming more and more
materialistic, it also increasingly allowed its concepts to be used
first by socialism and then by communism. So that Karl Marx was
able to say, in 1844, that "communism is naturalized humanism."

This statement has proved to be not entirely unreasonable. One does see the same stones in the foundations of an eroded humanism and of any type of socialism: boundless materialism; freedom from religion and religious responsibility (which under Communist regimes attains the stage of antireligious dictatorship); concentration on social structures with an allegedly scientific approach. (This last is typical of both the Age of Enlightenment and of Marxism.) It is no accident that all of communism's rhetorical vows resolve around Man (with a capital *M*) and his earthly happiness. At first glance it seems an ugly parallel: common traits in the thinking and way of life of today's West and today's East? But such is the logic of materialistic development.

The interrelationship is such, moreover, that the current of materialism which is farthest to the left, and is hence the most consistent, always proves to be stronger, more attractive, and victorious. Humanism which has lost its Christian heritage cannot prevail in this competition. Thus during the past centuries and especially in recent decades, as the process became more acute, the alignment of forces was as follows: Liberalism was inevitably pushed aside by radicalism, radicalism had to surrender to socialism, and socialism could not stand up to communism. The Communist regime in the East could endure and grow due to the enthusiastic support from an enormous number of Western intellectuals who (feeling the kinship!) refused to see communism's crimes, and when they no longer could do so, they tried to justify these crimes. The problem persists: In our Eastern countries, communism has suffered a complete ideological defeat; it is zero and less than zero. And yet Western intellectuals still look at it with considerable interest and empathy, and this is precisely what makes it so immensely difficult for the West to withstand the East.

Before the Turn

I am not examining the case of a disaster brought on by a world war and the changes which it would produce in society. But as long as we wake up every morning under a peaceful sun, we must lead an everyday life. Yet there is a disaster which is already very much with us. I am referring to the calamity of an autonomous, irreligious humanistic consciousness.

It has made man the measure of all things on earth—imperfect man, who is never free of pride, self-interest, envy, vanity, and dozens of other defects. We are now paying for the mistakes which were not properly appraised at the beginning of the journey. On the way from the Renaissance to our days we have enriched our experience, but we have lost the concept of a Supreme Complete Entity which used to restrain our passions and our irresponsibility. We have placed too much hope in politics and social reforms, only to find out that we were being deprived of our most precious possession: our spiritual life. It is trampled by the party mob in the East, by the commercial one in the West. This is the essence of the crisis: the split in the world is less terrifying than the similarity of the disease afflicting its main sections.

If, as claimed by humanism, man were born only to be happy, he would not be born to die. Since his body is doomed to death, his task on earth evidently must be more spiritual: not a total engrossment in everyday life, not the search for the best ways to obtain material goods and then their carefree consumption. It has to be the fulfillment of a permanent, earnest duty so that one's life journey may become above all an experience of moral growth: to leave life a better human being than one started it. It is imperative to reappraise the scale of the usual human values; its present incorrectness is astounding. It is not possible that assessment of the President's performance should be reduced to the question of how much money one makes or to the availability of gasoline. Only by the voluntary nurturing in ourselves of freely accepted and serene self-restraint can mankind rise above the world stream of materialism.

Today it would be retrogressive to hold on to the ossified formulas of the Enlightenment. Such social dogmatism leaves us helpless before the trials of our times.

Even if we are spared destruction by war, life will have to change in order not to perish on its own. We cannot avoid reassessing the fundamental definitions of human life and human society. Is it true that man is above everything? Is there no Superior

Spirit above him? Is it right that man's life and society's activities should be ruled by material expansion above all? Is it permissible to promote such expansion to the detriment of our integral spiritual life?

If the world has not approached its end, it has reached a major watershed in history, equal in importance to the turn from the Middle Ages to the Renaissance. It will demand from us a spiritual blaze; we shall have to rise to a new height of vision, to a new level of life, where our physical nature will not be cursed, as in the Middle Ages, but even more importantly, our spiritual being will not be trampled upon, as in the Modern Era.

This ascension is similar to climbing onto the next anthropological stage. No one on earth has any other way left but—upward.

PART TWO

EARLY RESPONSES

THE NEW YORK TIMES

The Obsession
of Solzhenitsyn

IF ANYONE HAS EARNED the right to call the West to a
moral reckoning, it is Aleksandr Solzhenitsyn. The high courage
and conviction which sustained him in the Soviet Gulag have
captured the admiration of all free people. So his criticisms of
America . . . compel attention and cut deep. Yes, our laws are
used by the rich and powerful to gain more wealth and power; our
press is often irresponsible; television is a swamp of nonsense;
pornography does flourish; and, yes, the nation is in thrall to
material things. But given all that, Mr. Solzhenitsyn's world view
seems to us far more dangerous than the easygoing spirit which he
finds so exasperating.

The argument he raises is not new; it goes back to the begin-
nings of the Republic and has never disappeared. At bottom, it is
the argument between the religious Enthusiasts, sure of their relationship to the Divine Will, and the men of the Enlightenment,
trusting in the rationality of humankind.

Although Mr. Solzhenitsyn comes out of a very different tradition, he has this in common with the Enthusiasts: he believes
himself to be in possession of The Truth and so sees error wherever he looks. The True Believer views the world as a conflict
between light and darkness, God and the Devil. Such a view can
be a source of great strength; it produces martyrs. To a Solzheni-

---

tsyn, the politicians of the West, forever weighing costs and benefits, forever trimming their ideals or trading them off, scarcely able to take a principled position and adhere to it, must seem like weaklings, if not scoundrels.

The trouble is, of course, that life in a society run by zealots like Mr. Solzhenitsyn is bound to be uncomfortable for those who do not share his vision or ascribe to his beliefs. Dissent was punished long before there was a gulag. It was in recognition of this simple but basic fact that the Founders took such pains to disperse power and safeguard individual freedoms. The high place accorded to the law—to which Mr. Solzhenitsyn heartily objects and which has indeed been mightily abused—has for 200 years protected Americans from arbitrary government.

As to this country's relations with the Communist states, we fear that Mr. Solzhenitsyn does the world no favor by calling up a holy war. The weapons are far too formidable, the stakes in human life far too high. But there is something else as well. Much as we have been instructed and inspired by Mr. Solzhenitsyn, his willingness to set aside all other values in the crusade against Communism bespeaks an obsession that we are happy to forgo in this nation's leaders. A certain amount of self-doubt is a valuable attribute for people who have charge of nuclear weapons.

Where Mr. Solzhenitsyn sees only softness and indecision in this country, we see something more—tolerance of many ideas, humility before the ultimate truths, a recognition of the responsibilities imposed by our awful power. When our leaders have departed from these quiet virtues, as in Vietnam, the result has been terrible damage, to others and to ourselves.

Mr. Solzhenitsyn has forced the West to see the full brutality of the Soviet regime, and has stiffened the resistance to Communism. Perhaps now that he is settled in America, he may come to learn that at least some of this nation's apparent weaknesses are precious and abiding strengths.

THE WASHINGTON POST

Mr. Solzhenitsyn as Witness

ALEXANDER SOLZHENITSYN'S PERSONAL credentials— as one who suffered and survived to bear artistic witness to the suffering of others—compel the closest attention to his public utterances. One cannot read his Harvard commencement address, however, without being reminded that it is not so much communism that is his enemy as the nature of modern man. The Renaissance, he believes, undermined the spiritual foundations of Western society as pervasively (though a bit more benevolently) as communism ravaged his native land. Spiritually, it has been pretty much downhill ever since. One part of the general failing is that the West has been unable to summon the courage to combat communism effectively. Then there is American music, which is "intolerable." The West, the author concludes, is unfit to be a model to "my country," Russia.

Well, Mr. Solzhenitsyn is not the first to detect spiritual flaws in the West. Yet he launches his critique from a position betraying a gross misunderstanding of Western society, which has chosen to organize its political and social and cultural affairs on the basis of a respect for the differences among men. In the vision that drives Alexander Solzhenitsyn, a divine force—or, to be more precise, a prophet such as himself—would provide the unifying inspiration for the whole society. And that force, or that prophet, would have available the authority needed to bring the vision to life.

This editorial appeared in the "Washington Post" on June 11, 1978, and is reprinted by permission.

Mr. Solzenitsyn's residence—temporary, he hopes—in the West has given him the opportunity to expound his views. But his views remain very Russian: They arise from particular religious and political strains remote from modern Western experience. If they explain anything, it is that there is a vast gap in tradition and perception between Westerners and many Russians—even, or especially, those who, like Mr. Solzhenitsyn, use the tolerance and diversity that are the splendors of the West to attack tolerance and diversity.

Mr. Solzhenitsyn's strictures on the lack of Western resolve will no doubt find their way promptly (and selectively) into the quivers of the American right, which is always searching for authentic witnesses to its own sense of embattlement with communism. But Mr. Solzhenitsyn is an unreliable witness. He appears to validate the common American concern for human rights. In fact, he carries that concern to an unacceptable extreme. It galls Mr. Solzhenitsyn to think that Western societies could contemplate coexisting with Soviet power. But it is precisely because he speaks at a moment of aroused anxiety about Kremlin purpose that one must emphasize that he is summoning Americans to a crusade.

For the West, respect for diversity has an international dimension as well as an individual one. If Mr. Solzhenitsyn understands this, he does not accept it. He speaks for boundless cold war.

THE WASHINGTON STAR

Solzhenitsyn at Harvard

IT IS PROBABLY A MEASURE of their disquieting accuracy that Alexander Solzhenitsyn's periodic castigations of Western humanist values cry out for sharp rebuttal. He was back in the pulpit last week at the Harvard commencement; and the urge to respond sharply and defensively is, as usual, overpowering.

One's immediate instinct is to ask how much a Russian novelist living out his days behind a high fence, in an isolated Vermont village, *really* knows about the vibrant pluralistic society he finds so miserably deficient in spirituality. It is to recall that a cranky puritanism is the classic affliction of great Russian men of letters; that few of them, with the exception of Turgenev, have ever been of ironic, tolerant or self-critical temperament; that even Tolstoy, the greatest of all, ended his life in sour disgust with human variety and even with his own art, having concluded that all of it was vanity and frivolity.

Solzhenitsyn certainly needs placing in this tradition, for it explains quite a bit about his own jaundiced view of the world to which he came four years ago as an unwilling exile. Yet merely to establish the context of the matter is not to grapple responsibly with the matter itself.

What, to begin with, is he actually saying? The most familiar of his themes is, of course, that the liberal, skeptical pluralistic values of the West dangerously blind it to the relentlessness and

---

This editorial appeared in the "Washington Star" on June 11, 1978, and is reprinted by permission.

evil of totalitarian ambitions—that we make fools of ourselves by attributing our own benevolent purposes to those who have very different ones. There is disturbing truth in this; it is a worry that we must live with; but the remedy is never obvious. Is it not among the deadliest of many "totalitarian temptations" that free societies might adopt, in self-defense, the very character they set out to defend themselves against?

But politics and strategy are far from being the central feature of Mr. Solzhenitsyn's message. His prophecy isn't, in the strictest sense, political and in some respects is indeed anti-political. It belongs to other realms: historical, aesthetic, religious.

Historically, it is an attack on the fundamental shift of values which we traditionally associate with the Renaissance, in which the classical world's exalted estimate of the human personality was rediscovered and made the measure of things. Aesthetically, it is a keen and puritanical distaste for the frivolous and debased standards of popular culture—"TV stupor," as he calls it, and "intolerable music" and a pervasive commercialism that contaminates every purpose with a sales pitch of some kind. Religiously, it is the belief, quite pronounced in a sensitive Russian who has looked into the depths of the Stalinist hell, that the peoples of the West simply haven't suffered enough; that their dross is not sufficiently purged by misery.

These obsessions touch upon, but do not satisfactorily elaborate, complex truths about the West. They can't be dismissed with the mere protest that Mr. Solzhenitsyn dwells too much on the dark side and misses many concealed dimensions of seriousness—though that is also true.

In fact, in these highly subjective realms of perception, rebuttal as such is idle. There is no disputing spiritual perceptions, or tastes. Yet the great Russian prophet in our midst probably exaggerates Western decadence; and he certainly scants the complex value of free political and economic systems.

Such systems cannot, in their nature, refine or even predictably direct the tastes and moral purposes to which they give free play. Regimentation, for good or ill, is not their purpose. What Mr. Solzhenitsyn sees as spiritual chaos and vulgarity is the inescapable consequence of our view that the state is not, and cannot be, the appointed teacher of people. That is a role we reserve for private institutions—the church, the school, the family. It is their strengths or weaknesses that are reflected in the decay and confusion Mr. Solzhenitsyn deplores; it is to their strengthening that free peoples look for "spiritual" regeneration.

The West, says Mr, Solzhenitsyn, is not today an appealing model for the spiritual rebirth of the totalitarian nations. To which the right answer is: *Of course it isn't—and can't be*. Those who are regimented in an evil and soul-destroying system will not find an alternative model of regimentation by looking west.

They *will* find, however, a system that affords human nature the opportunity to declare itself freely, in all its glory and its sordidness.

NATIONAL REVIEW

Thoughts
on Solzhenitsyn

IN ITS JULY 7 ISSUE, *NR* published the full translated text of Aleksandr Solzhenitsyn's Harvard commencement address. Solzhenitsyn is a towering presence on the landscape of twentieth century literature and politics, and this address is likely to be read, pondered, and discussed a century hence. Those who heard it there, and those who discuss it in its own historical moment, are specially privileged.

In many of his central contentions. Solzhenitsyn is self-evidently correct, a courageous man, and a prophet willing to split the twentieth century like an old tin can, reopening the enduring questions of political and religious thought.

At the same time, Solzhenitsyn surrounds his profound truths with sometimes strident claims and assertions that distract attentive listeners from his deepest insights. The English translation of his address is seriously flawed. In due course, *NR* will endeavor to provide a more accurate and nuanced version. Nevertheless, reading what we do have now, some doubts arise on the margins of his central message.

Solzhenitsyn's main contentions can scarcely be gainsaid.

In the Vietnam War, "the American intelligentsia lost its nerve." The "members of the U.S. antiwar movement wound up being involved in the betrayal of Far Eastern nations, in a

---

This editorial appeared in "National Review" on July 21, 1978, and is reprinted by permission (© 1978 by National Review Incorporated).

genocide, and in the suffering today imposed on thirty million people there." Can there be any argument at all with those statements?

Also, Solzhenitsyn is willing to say the unsayable, i.e., that Hitler was not the most dangerous of all political evils, that a worse one existed: "Western democracy cultivated another enemy who would prove worse and more powerful yet: Hitler never had so many resources and so many people, nor did he offer any attractive ideas, or have such a large number of supporters in the West." True. But with the caveat that Hitler seems to have won the war of ideas in the Third World, where most regimes are surely "national socialist."

Solzhenitsyn is profoundly right in his assertion that national and civilizational survival is a matter of will: "No weapons, no matter how powerful, can help the West until it overcomes its loss of will power." And such will power, many would agree with Solzhenitsyn, has theological roots, and is connected with faith and hope.

Nevertheless, surrounding these core assertions are others, arguable, dubious, or self-evidently false, which detract from the power of the central Solzhenitsyn witness.

1. Is it true, and this is a deep question, that "truth seldom is pleasant; it is almost invariably bitter"? Quite possibly. But Dante refers repeatedly to "the sweet world," and Dante was no child of illusion.

2. Is it true that Western material abundance interferes with "free spiritual development"? By all available indices, the Western world is in the midst of a religious revival, both within and outside of orthodox channels. If abundance is in fact the enemy of the spirit—well, in comparison with what alternative circumstances, either in space or in time?

3. Is it really true that the Russian people have been purged by suffering, and are less materialistic and spiritually stronger than their Western counterparts? To the external gaze, at least, the average Russian seems preoccupied with material things, and the opposite of courageous.

4. Is it credible to describe life in the U.S. and the West in

general as ruled purely by formal laws? "If one is right from a legal point of view, nothing more is required. . . . Everybody operates at the extreme limit of the legal frames." Is that *true? Everybody?*

5. Is it true that the press, meaning all the media, is "the greatest power within the Western countries, more powerful than the legislature, the executive, and the judiciary"? Possibly, but the assessment cannot simply be asserted.

6. Is it really true that "what is not fashionable will hardly ever find its way into periodicals or books or be heard in colleges"? Counter question: Have you read this far in this editorial?

Solzhenitsyn's great power resides in his relentless fidelity to the truth. At his best, he can say with Walt Whitman, "I am the man, I suffered, I was there." His major novels, and his great act of historical recovery, *The Gulag Archipelago,* derive their authority from his sense of fact, and his reverence for it. Suspect assertions and faulty translation can only erode such authority.

GEORGE F. WILL

Solzhenitsyn's Critics

ALEXANDER SOLZHENITSYN RESEMBLES both the dove in Genesis that found no rest, and the prophets who allowed no rest. As a prophet should, he has, with his Harvard commencement address, stirred a reaction that reveals the complacency of society.

The West, he says, has advanced socially "in accordance with its proclaimed intentions," so its thinness of spirit is evidence of a mistake "at the very basis" of thinking in recent centuries. When modern civilization based itself on the "worship [of] man and his material needs," then "Everything beyond physical well-being and accumulation of material goods, all other human requirements and characteristics of a subtler and higher nature, were left outside the arena of attention of state and social systems, as if human life did not have any superior sense."

During the early ascendance of modern thinking, says Solzhenitsyn, the West was sustained by the spiritual legacy of the preceding millennium. Mankind was understood to have been "endowed" (to use the language of the Declaration of Independence) with certain rights by God, so "freedom was given to the individual conditionally, in the assumption of his constant religious responsibility." Subsequently, "We have placed too much hope in political and social reforms, only to find out that we were deprived of our most precious possession: our spiritual life."

The New York Times, whose spacious skepticism extends to all values except its own, considers Solzhenitsyn "dangerous"

GEORGE F. WILL *is a syndicated columnist with the Washington Post Writers Group. This article appeared in June 1978 and is reprinted by permission.*

and a "zealot" because "he believes himself to be in possession of The Truth." The Times wishes he were more like the American Founders who, The Times forgets, committed treason and waged an eight-year war on behalf of The Truth they considered "self-evident."

The Washington Post says Solzhenitsyn's views are "very Russian: They arise from particular religious and political strains remote from modern Western experience."

They are, indeed, unmodern, even anti-modern, but they are not exclusively Russian. His ideas about the nature of man and the essential political problem are broadly congruent with the ideas of Cicero and other ancients, and those of Augustine, Aquinas, Richard Hooker, Pascal, Thomas More, Burke, Hegel and others.

Compared to the long and broad intellectual tradition in which Solzhenitsyn's views are rooted, the tradition of modernity, or liberalism, is short and thin.

The Times, which accuses Solzhenitsyn of interpreting the world in terms of a crude dichotomy, interprets Solzhenitsyn in terms of an "argument between the religious Enthusiasts, sure of their relationship to the Divine Will, and the men of the Enlightenment, trusting in the rationality of mankind." The Post says Solzhenitsyn betrays "a gross misunderstanding of Western society, which has chosen to organize its political and social and cultural affairs on the basis of a respect for the differences among men."

But there is another, less congratulatory, more accurate and quite opposite interpretation of the modern political tradition.

Modern politics emphasizes the sameness, not the diversity, of people. It seeks to found stable societies on the lowest, commonest, strongest passion: self interest that is tamed by being turned to economic pursuits.

In such societies, law does not point people toward elevated lives. The law's only purpose is to organize and encourage a taming materialism. Modern politics assumes that it is not virtue that makes people free, but freedom that makes people virtuous, at least if virtue is defined as pursuit of pleasure in accordance with minimal legality.

Such a society asks and receives little self-restraint and civic spirit, and produces what Solzhenitsyn calls "an atmosphere of moral mediocrity, paralyzing man's noblest impulses." Solzhenitsyn doubts that a society founded on lightly regulated selfishness can summon the vision and sacrifice necessary for combating determined enemies.

De Tocqueville, Henry Adams, Irving Babbitt, Paul Elmer More, Peter Viereck and others constitute a submerged but continuous tradition that shares Solzhenitsyn's anxiety about American premises and the culture they produce. And Solzhenitsyn's philosophy has a far more distinguished pedigree than does the liberalism that is orthodoxy in societies that owe their success, so far, to the fact that they have lived off the moral capital of older and sounder traditions, capital that is a wasting asset.

America's flaccid consensus about its premises is a study in intellectual parochialism. That consensus lacks the intellectual weight to justify Solzhenitsyn's critics in being as dismissive as they are about his restatement of the most ancient and honorable theme of Western political philosophy.

JAMES RESTON

A Russian at Harvard

ALEKSANDR SOLZHENITSYN SAID SO MANY true and even noble things in his address to the Harvard graduates a few days ago that one wonders why he spoiled his message with so many unfair, provocative, and even silly comparisons on the side.

His attack on the materialism and moral squalor of the Western nations and their selfish subversion of freedom was fair enough.

"Even if we are spared destruction by war," he told the Harvard graduates, "our lives will have to change if we want to save life from self-destruction. We cannot avoid revising the fundamental definitions of human life and human society.

"Is it true that man is above everything? Is there no Superior Spirit above him? Is is right that man's life and society's activities have to be determined by material expansion? Is it permissible to promote such expansion to the detriment of our spiritual integrity. . . ?"

These are good questions, which the poet Archibald MacLeish raises with equal eloquence and better balance in his latest book of essays and reflections, "Riders on the Earth." But Mr. Solzhenitsyn went beyond questions to conclusions that made Oswald Spengler's "Decline of the West" sound recklessly optimistic.

Mr. Solzenitsyn talked of "a decline in courage" as perhaps the most striking feature of the Western world today—not only in the United States but in all free nations, particularly among all the political leaders and the intellectual elites.

JAMES RESTON *is a columnist for the "New York Times," where this article appeared on June 11, 1978 (© 1978 by the New York Times Company; reprinted by permission).*

Our leaders bullied weak countries, he suggested, but were "tongue-tied and paralyzed when they deal with powerful governments and threatening forces, with aggressors and international terrorists."

To be fair, Mr. Solzhenitsyn, who was exiled from the Soviet Union four years ago for his criticism of the brutality and inhumanity of the Soviet political system, emphasized that he was not recommending that system as a substitute for the weaknesses in the West. But he added:

"I could not recommend your society such as it is today as a model for the transformation of ours. Through intense suffering, our country [the Soviet Union] has now achieved a spiritual development of such intensity that the Western system in its present state of spiritual exhaustion does not look attractive.

"A fact which cannot be disputed is the weakening of human beings in the West while in the East they are becoming firmer and stronger. Six decades for our [Russian] people and three decades for the people of Eastern Europe; during that time we have been through a spiritual training far in advance of Western experience. . . ."

This from the author of the unspeakable tortures of the Soviet prisons and psychiatric wards? This is "a fact which cannot be disputed"? The hell it can't. Mr. Solzhenitsyn entitled his commencement address at Harvard "A World Split Apart," but for all its brilliant passages, it sounded like the wanderings of a mind split apart.

He suggests that it was the spiritual bankruptcy and physical cowardice of the United States that led to what he calls "the hasty Vietnam capitulation." Hasty? After a generation of slaughter? Lack of courage? It was precisely because the American people still heard some echoes of their spiritual heritage and belief in the sanctity of individual human life that they rose up against the genocide Mr. Solzhenitsyn condemns.

There is a fundamental contradiction in this Solzhenitsyn speech. For on the one hand he argues that "only moral criteria can help the West against Communism's strategy," but on the other, that only American military power and willpower could have stopped the carnage in Vietnam by continuing it, and avoiding the expansion of Communist power in Asia.

It is an interesting argument, particularly since it was made when the domino theory doesn't seem to be working in Southeast Asia; when the Cambodian Communists and the Vietnam Communists are fighting each other; when Hanoi is driving the Chinese back into the People's Republic; and when all the fears at the end of the Vietnam war have not come to pass.

Anyway, as commencement speeches go, there is something to be said for Mr. Solzhenitsyn. He was right to complain that "hastiness and superficiality are the psychic disease of the Twentieth Century." He had some good tough criticisms to make of the press, even though he sounded in the process a little like Spiro Agnew, and he said some true and poignant things.

"After the suffering of decades of violence and oppression, the human soul longs for things higher, warmer and purer than those offered by today's mass living habits, introduced by the revolting invasion of publicity, by TV stupor and by intolerable music."

But at least he was allowed to say all these things. On commencement day at Moscow University, if they have one, the "spiritual superiority" of the Soviet Union probably wouldn't have allowed it.

OLGA ANDREYEV CARLISLE

Solzhenitsyn's
Invisible Audience

LIKE THE RUMBLE OF an early summer storm, Aleksandr Solzhenitsyn's commencement speech at Harvard resounded throughout the United States. Russia's greatest writer, now living out his exile in the seclusion of Vermont, had at last broken a silence of more than two years, and his message and his rhetoric suited the occasion perfectly. America's most celebrated guest sounded like a fire-and-brimstone preacher out of the Puritan era, like a latter-day Cotton Mather. Solzhenitsyn's indictment of the corruption in the West echoed America's own doubts about its moral, social and political predicaments today.

Salvation, Solzhenitsyn was saying, lies in asceticism, in renouncing frivolity and materialism and the persistent pursuit of happiness. In particular, he was scornful of our free press, a legacy from the age of the Founding Fathers which has been perverted by our godlessness.

As an American of Russian descent who, working in secret, had arranged for the publication of two of Solzhenitsyn's books in the West while he was still in the Soviet Union, I was deeply intrigued by what I saw as Solzhenitsyn's transformation since I first met him in 1967. Most Russians driven from their country by Soviet

OLGA ANDREYEV CARLISLE *is a painter and writer who helped to get two of Solzhenitsyn's books published in the West before he left the Soviet Union. This article appeared in "Newsweek," July 24, 1978, and is reprinted by permission (© 1978 by Newsweek, Incorporated; all rights reserved).*

intolerance have seen Solzhenitsyn as a champion of freedom and the right of all to know the truth. Yet now he was saying that an unbridled press is intolerable:"[In the West] 'everyone is entitled to know everything.' But this is a false slogan, characteristic of a false era: people also have the right not to know, and it is a much more valuable one." It did not occur to him that he owed his own opportunity to speak out on that day to generations of Americans who shaped and preserved those liberties Russia has never had, the secular liberties formulated in the eighteenth century, particularly freedom of speech and of the press.

And then, as I listened, another meaning emerged. Solzhenitsyn, the spokesman for a new, ascetic religiosity, was addressing his U.S. audience only incidentally. He was really speaking to the Soviet leaders and to the Russian people. He wanted them to know he had not been seduced by the false values of the West. His soul is still Russian. If only the Soviets would forsake Marxism—in his view another accursed, though indirect, inheritance from the Age of Englightenment—then Mother Russia, healed by religion and a new moral order, could be reborn.

Solzhenitsyn is not alone in dreaming of this rebirth. Many members of the Soviet Establishment, disappointed by the human and economic failures of Communism, share his yearnings. They want a strong Russia, untainted by alien ideologies, with her patriarchal values restored. These aspirations are shared by many within the Russian masses who are aware of the drabness and emptiness of their daily lives and blame this on "foreigners." The fact that the Soviet Union encompasses many non-Russian nationalities, whose birthrates far exceed that of the Russians, worries them. They draw on Russia's most ancient and persistent myth, Russian nationalism, the belief that the Russians are a chosen people, bearer of a higher truth.

As the present leadership ages, concerns about the future mount; new political alternatives must be found. The *Russity*, as the new Russian nationalists are sometimes known, are becoming more influential. Secretly they hold the Marxist ideology in contempt. They despise the present-day atheistic Soviet intelligentsia. They are anti-Semitic. They are to be found in all layers of the

Soviet hierarchy, most particularly within the military and the KGB.

To the observers of today's Soviet Union, the Russity's ascendancy is unmistakable. For example, the painter Ilya Glazunov, the iconographer of this movement, has at last, after twenty years, been given a major one-man show. Thousands stand in line to see his paintings of Russian saints and national heroes. He is said to be a Russian patriot who believes that, after 60 years of Soviet power, the Russian people are the most disadvantaged of the more than 100 nationalities in the Soviet Union. In Moscow, Glazunov is commonly regarded as an anti-Semite and a KGB official.

One must not confuse the Russity with the thousands upon thousands in the Soviet Union who are showing a renewed interest in religion. Russian Orthodoxy has always included both men of true religiosity and activists determined to use the church for political purposes. The Russity belong to the latter category.

In the last ten years, many Soviet dissenters have gradually shifted to the right. It is as if their increasing familiarity with life in the West, the result of détente and emigration, has caused them to draw back, to seek paths to social justice other than those of the West, which they see as tainted by materialism and amorality. The alternative favored by Solzhenitsyn is a benevolently autocratic, religious state, which voluntarily would grant its citizens a limited freedom. In it, inner freedom is emphasized at the expense of civil liberties. Little consideration is given to the creation of a system of checks and balances which alone could keep such a social order from becoming tyrannical.

The new dissenting right emphasizes Russia's future role as the embodiment of a strong, purified Orthodoxy: her very suffering at the hands of godless Communism mystically predestines her for this leading role, a role vital in a world where both capitalism and Marxism are on the verge of collapse. It is the conviction of this new Russian right that greater attention should be paid to China, which is suspected of coveting Russian territories. There are not many years left during which the Soviet Union can be certain of winning a war with China; traditionally having an enemy at the gate is the surest way to awake national feelings. For this reason, nothing is more threatening to Russia than a potential Sino-American rapprochement which would strengthen the enemy.

Solzhenitsyn is not deliberately stirring nationalistic feelings in his homeland, yet instinctively he is in sympathy with such sentiments. His own convictions are deeply rooted in the Russian spirit, which is untempered by the civilizing influences of a democratic tradition. Should a new right ever come into its own in the Soviet Union, Solzhenitsyn, one of Russia's prophets, might well return home in triumph.

JACK FRUCHTMAN, JR.

A Voice From Russia's Past at Harvard

ALEXANDER SOLZHENITSYN'S HARVARD University commencement address seems to have perplexed and annoyed more than it has enlightened. Some people, like New York *Times* columnist James Reston, have noted that what Mr. Solzhenitsyn said about Western decadence is self-evident: everyone knows about our excessive preoccupation with material things and our difficulty in grappling with many moral issues.

The question which ought to be asked is what motivated Mr. Solzhenitsyn. Why did he offer this indictment of Western society, and then suggest really nothing in the way of a remedy? In all fairness, he did seem to point obliquely and indeterminately to a remedy when he spoke of a hoped-for regeneration of Western "spiritual life."

This choice of phraseology ("spiritual life") and indeed his choice of language throughout his address and much of his writings is extremely suggestive of the Russian past. For to understand Mr. Solzhenitsyn at Harvard, one must have some knowledge of a mid-19th Century group of Russian romantic intellectuals who developed a comprehensive (though hardly systematic) ideology centered on the historical mission of Russia and the Orthodox Church.

JACK FRUCHTMAN, JR., *is a free-lance writer and a visiting professor in the Department of History at Johns Hopkins University. This article appeared in the "Baltimore Sun" on June 18, 1978, and is reprinted by permission.*

43

This group of individuals, collectively known as the "Slavo-philes," was loosely organized, but bound together by family ties and friendships. It never possessed a formal organization, and it never exerted intellectual or philosophical conformity on its members.

In his Harvard address, Mr. Solzhenitsyn sounds very much like a 19th-Century Slavophile.

The term "Slavophile" originally was probably a term of deri-sion applied in the early 19th Century to a group of Russian philologists and nationalists interested in the origins of the Rus-sian language. Slavophiles proper were most active at mid-century. Led principally by Alexis Khomiakov and Ivan Kiereev-sky, the Slavophiles believed that the West, because of its pecul-iar historical development, had entered into spiritual decline and that it could be saved by a regenerating Russian spiritual influence.

Mr. Solzhenitsyn echoed this theme at Harvard when he noted that the philosophical foundation of the West has historically rested on a "rationalistic humanism," by which he meant "the proclaimed and enforced autonomy of man from any higher force above him." This notion directly reflected the Slavophile doctrine that the decline of the West has occurred because Westerners have never truly realized that man was essentially a spiritual or religious, rather than a rational or material, being. "We turned our backs upon the Spirit," Mr. Solzhenitsyn proclaimed, "and em-braced all that is material with excessive and unwarranted zeal."

The Slavophiles condemned the West precisely for this same reason. The West, they argued, had emphasized rationality, com-pulsion and above all legalistic institutions and material well-being. Each of these qualities was in conflict with man's inherent goodness and virtue.

For the Slavophiles, the West was decadent primarily because it had adopted the worship of rationality, matter and form. Moreover, it relied too much on legalistic systems of thought and action. This emphasis on the rational and on the legalistic, they thought, had originated in Rome which had passed it on to the Catholic Church. From the church, it was a short distance for them to be absorbed by Protestantism, from where it spread throughout Western culture and society.

In his address, Mr. Solzhenitsyn spoke of the inordinate Western propensity for rationalism (hence, his reference to rationalistic humanism). In addition, he decried our legalistic system as indicative of Western cowardice and weakness: "a society with no other scale but the legal one is not quite worthy of man." He went on in his indictment in a manner which probably would have received the assent of his Slavophile predecessors: "whenever the tissue of life is woven of legalistic relations," he said, "there is an atmosphere of moral mediocrity, paralyzing man's noblest impulses."

Unlike the Slavophiles, who had dated the origin of this decline from ancient Rome, Mr. Solzhenitsyn saw it as beginning only in the Renaissance. But either way, both Mr. Solzhenitsyn and the Slavophiles believe that this decline and everything accompanying it was deeply rooted in Western history, a history of man, where man has lost his spiritual tie to the infinite, the eternal, and the timeless. The Slavophile Ivan Kiereevsky wrote that "it is painful to see what a subtle, but inevitable and just-sent madness now drives the Western man. He feels his darkness, and, like a moth, he flies into the fire, which he takes to be the sun. He cries like a frog and barks like a dog, when he hears the Word of God." Man, in short, is no longer human, and the decline of the West is upon us.

For both Mr. Solzhenitsyn and the Slavophiles, then, man's spiritual capacities have become subverted by the overpowering influences of reason and legality. This influence has led to the rise of specific instances of decadence and degeneration which Mr. Solzhenitsyn enumerated in his address: moral cowardice, especially in our dealings with Communist regimes and in our retreat from Vietnam; materialism and the complacency it has inspired in people; sharp legal maneuvering; a press which invades privacy and which acts as an unperceived censor; our television-caused stupor and our intolerable music. When Mr. Solzhenitsyn spoke of "the forces of evil" which "have begun their decisive offensive," he was not directly referring to a sudden surge of sin or to an appearance of demons. He meant, more particularly, that just as the earlier Slavophiles complained, we have passed from our former days when the West was "the land of holy miracles" (as Khomiakov put it) to a time when we have lost our "willpower."

These specific instances signify our decline. We are confronted with a society of our own making, a society with which we may feel generally comfortable, but only because we live it every day. But for Mr. Solzhenitsyn, it is a society which is doomed because of its rejection of spirituality and its concomitant worship of reason and material things. We are indeed a Godless people, we in the West.

Mr. Solzhenitsyn's evaluation of the West was, then, fairly close to the analysis of the West given by the Slavophiles. They, of course, had no real fear of the final doom of the Western world, because Russia was going to renew the entire world spiritually.

Russia was different, because she embodied that fundamental spirituality that the Slavophiles (and Mr. Solzhenitsyn) found so lacking in the West. Clearly, Russia was far from being the perfect country. Just as Mr. Solzhenitsyn rejected the idea of the West as a model for the transformation of the Soviet Union, so the Slavophiles also acknowledged that Russia was not quite prepared to be the spiritual paradigm of the West.

Not yet, at any rate. As it is, however, things were decidedly better in Russia, according to the Slavophiles. Russian society was based on strong familial ties, and it had the institution of the peasant commune which bound people together into a harmonious, organic unity. Above all, it possessed Orthodoxy, the true Christian expression of Jesus's life and teaching. (Need we remind ourselves of Mr. Solzhenitsyn's Orthodoxy?)

Russia, for the Slavophiles, was spiritually, if not economically, socially and politically, powerful. As Ivan Kiereevsky wrote in the last century: "Russia is a different story; she experienced no struggle, no conquest, no eternal war, no endless treaties; she is not a creation of circumstance, but the product of a living, organic development; she has not been constructed, she grew." Russia collectively embodied the ideal spirit of love, freedom, harmony and peace.

But where must Mr. Solzhenitsyn turn, especially when his

own beloved Russia has exiled him? Midway through his address to the Harvard graduates, he offered an answer to this very question. First, he distinguished the true Russia from the Soviet Communist state. At Harvard, he reiterated his belief that the Soviets have attempted (and to him it is only an attempt) to destroy the Russian soul, Russian spirituality, "by the dealings and machinations of the ruling party."

But the Russian spirit, he says, is not destroyed. In fact, the situation is quite the opposite. As the Slavophiles heralded Russian spirituality vis-à-vis Western materialism, so did Mr. Solzhenitsyn: "Through intense suffering," he said, "our country [Russia] has now achieved a spiritual development of such intensity that the Western system in its present state of physical exhaustion does not look attractive." Under the Communist yoke ("six decades for our people, three decades for the people of Eastern Europe"), "we have been through a spiritual training far in advance of Western experience. Life's complexity and mortal weight have produced stronger, deeper and more interesting characters than those generated by standarized Western well-being."

His point by now should be clear to all of us: Russia—true Russia—will rise to be the salvation of the world, as the Slavophiles had taught over 100 years ago. Russia—not in spite of, but because of its horrible suffering for the past 60 years—has the sustenance, the religio-spiritual sustenance, to save the world, and especially the West, from its own depleted self.

Placed in this Slavophilic context, Mr. Solzhenitsyn's address makes a great deal of sense. While we may be aghast at the forcefulness of his indictment, we are still left with the problem of having to confront the specific issues which he has raised. The challenge for us in the West is not to construct an argument against the content of his address. Nor is it necessarily to fight Communist takeovers in Vietnam or anywhere else that Mr. Solzhenitsyn says we should. Our true challenge is with ourselves: To overcome the failings and the weaknesses in our Western way of life. This is where Mr. Solzhenitsyn's anguish over the lack of Western moral thinking and spirituality perhaps rings truest.

CHARLES KESLER

Up From Modernity

IT WAS STARTLING, sitting there with the graduating class that expected, and alumni who remembered, the traditional commencement pieties, to hear an address that began, *"Harvard's motto is* Veritas," and then proceeded—not to a eulogy of Harvard, but to a sobering examination of *Veritas*. Truth, after all—the very idea that there is such a thing as objective truth—is not much at home on college campuses these days. Once or twice a year it is invited to class, but only to be dismissed as dogged superstition, or debunked as a sort of grand Ptolemaic error. Never mind the paradox that the denial of truth has itself to be true: Solzhenitsyn was arresting because he spoke of the truth as if it *were* true.

Nothing Solzhenitsyn said at Harvard, however, was as startling as what his critics thought he had said. In general they accused him of what the *Washington Post,* for instance, called "a gross misunderstanding of Western society," though they were disagreed as to why he had misunderstood it. A few—you will find them in any crowd—thought him just plain bonkers: James Reston declared that Solzhenitsyn's address (titled "A World Split Apart"), "for all its brilliant passages, . . . sounded like the wanderings of a mind split apart." But most opted for cultural determinism and charitably pronounced Solzhenitsyn to be, well, incorrigibly Russian. His views "arise from particular religious and political strains remote from Western experience," the *Post* said sniffily. Really imaginative commentators espied a theocrat;

CHARLES KESLER *is a graduate student in political science at Harvard University. This article appeared in "National Review," September 15, 1978, and is reprinted by permission (© 1978 by National Review Incorporated).*

and the *New York Times* proclaimed him a "zealot" preaching "holy war," who, like the eighteenth century "religious Enthusiasts . . . believes himself to be in possession of The Truth and sees error [c'mon guys: that should've been "Error"] wherever he looks."

Diverse though they are, these critics have one thing in common: they believe themselves to be in possession of The Truth about Solzhenitsyn. In fact they miss his whole point.

A World Split Apart

Of course it is difficult for journalists who learned in college that all values are relative, and who remain awestruck by that truth, to weigh the heretical claim that all values may *not* be relative. But that is precisely what one must do, if only for a moment, in order to understand what Solzhenitsyn is trying to say. To understand requires that one first respect the author's terms; and that means, *inter alia,* paying attention to things like—the title of his address. Solzhenitsyn spoke of "A World Split Apart," even though, strictly speaking, his discussion of "worlds" occupies only a few paragraphs. A moment's reflection on the title provides a key to the full measure of Solzhenitsyn's indictment of modern society. For Solzhenitsyn's critics have dismissed him as illiberal without realizing that, in truth, he is *anti-modern;* that his doubts about the modern enterprise are fundamental, comprehensive; that he is asking, not merely, Is there a way out of Communism? but, Is there a way out of modernity? Or more precisely, Is there a way *up* from modernity?

1. The first meaning of the speech's title is easily recognizable as a vision of contemporary politics. *"Even at a hasty glance,"* Solzhenitsyn says—which is to say, even as journalists and other modern men routinely see things—it is obvious that two great superpowers oppose each other across the globe. But this *"political conception"* reflects only a partial understanding of the world, one that crystallizes in the *"illusion that danger may be abolished through successful diplomatic negotiations or by achieving a balance of armed forces."*

2. In truth, *"The split is a much profounder and more alienating one . . ."* whose nature begins to become apparent only when one considers how the split is usually expressed in speech. The United States and its philosophical allies proclaim a belief in "human rights" of the sort embodied in the Declaration of Independence—natural rights—and hold them to be the basis of civil government. Government exists to secure these rights, to protect the conditions of the pursuit of happiness. The Soviet Union and its allies call themselves Marxists. What exactly this means is the sort of question that exercises scholars over lifetimes, but it means at least a rejection of the idea of an unchanging human nature—and hence of natural rights. It is understood that Marxists believe in History or dialectical materialism, which is to say they believe that over time man changes his nature, that he creates himself, as it were, through his labor in time, and that the history of this creation through labor is the history of class struggle.

There is then a philosophical as well as a political division between West and East; or, one might say, a moral division, taking into account both the philosophical difference and the nature of its effect on political conduct. The so-called convergence theory, which tends to be widely discussed in the brief stretches between Soviet atrocities, concentrates on the lowest things—common bureaucratic and technological means, common scientific ends—and so misses the higher, and essential, difference between the U.S. and the USSR. This gulf is not economic, but moral and philosophical. So there is a philosophical split in the modern world or, *mutatis mutandis,* a split within the world of modern philosophy.

3. Very tidy—but doesn't a look around the globe reveal more cracks than we've allowed for? *"There is the concept of the Third World,"* Solzhenitsyn continues; *"thus, we already have three worlds. Undoubtedly; however, the number is even greater; we are just too far away to see."* If any *"ancient, deeply rooted, autonomous culture . . . constitutes an autonomous world,"* then China, India, Africa, and pre-revolutionary Russia, for example, must also be counted.

A Decline in Courage

Still, there is a sense in which these countries *are* part of the modern world, inasmuch as the very idea of Third and Fourth Worlds is a modern idea. Third World nations are called developing nations for a reason, after all; they are developing *into* something; they are, to use the totem-word of an entire social science discipline, "modernizing." It would not take much thought to connect the distinction between modern and developing worlds to the distinction between modern (or "rational-legal") and traditional societies, a distinction that emerged in late nineteenth century social science—most memorably in the work of Max Weber, whose books have been to sociology roughly what the Authorized Version has been to Protestantism. The division or *split* of the world into developed and developing halves—like the division into democratic and Communist—is an outgrowth of modern philosophy and social science. Neither of these splits transcends the modern viewpoint that Solzhenitsyn is engaged in identifying and refuting.

While it's true that the distinction between modern and traditional is not the same thing as a wish or expectation that the traditional should give way to the modern, in practice the one often elides into the other. In the West's *"blindness of superiority,"* remarks Solzhenitsyn, the notion is born that *"vast regions everywhere on our planet should develop and mature to the level of present-day Western systems. . . . There is this belief that all those other worlds are only being temporarily prevented by wicked governments or by heavy crimes or by their own barbarity and incomprehension from taking the way of Western pluralistic democracy. . . ."* The modern taxonomy of traditional and modern *"developed out of Western incomprehension of the essence of other worlds."* It judges countries *"on the basis of their progress"* toward modernity without questioning what sort of modernity (e.g., Western or Eastern) is the end of progress, or indeed whether modernity as a whole is choiceworthy.

4. *"A decline in courage,"* Solzhenitsyn declares, *"may be the most striking feature which an outside observer notices in the*

West in our days. The Western world has lost its civic courage. . . ." Although this loss is recent and might appear to be adventitious, Solzhenitsyn attributes it to the dynamics of the *"prevailing Western view of the world"* that was born in the Renaissance and *"found its political expression starting in the . . . Enlightenment."* What distinguished this view of the world was a tremendous burst of *"human independence and power"* and a radical new conception of science. For centuries science had been regarded as essentially contemplative, existing for the sake of understanding. Modern science exists for the sake of human power. When it first burst upon the world it was arrogant, impatient, ambitious—and frightfully exciting, for it promised revolutionary results. For two thousand years philosophers had sought to understand the world; the point now was to master and change it. Science, designed to serve (in Bacon's shining phrase) for the "relief of man's estate," promised affluence; affluence, a society at once happier and more just, as the motives for injustice were overcome.

In the last few decades, *"technical and social progress has permitted the realization of such aspirations. . . . The majority of people have been granted well-being to an extent their fathers and grandfathers could not even dream about . . . an almost unlimited freedom of enjoyment."* However, the concentration on material well-being has jeopardized the way to *"free spiritual development."* Man is in danger of not only winning the world but losing his soul; he may soon discover that without his soul it is impossible to keep the world. If modern society is organized around the paramount natural right of self-preservation, as, for instance, Hobbes, Locke, and Madison understood it to be, then why should a citizen risk his *"precious life in defense of common values"?*

The Letter of the Law

Modernity began as an effort to improve society by enlarging man's power and dominion over nature. In politics, the means of improvement it characteristically adopted were institutions and laws, which it invested with the confidence of Kant's bold asseveration that just government "is only a question of the good organization of the state. . . . The problem of organizing a state, however hard it may seem, can be solved even for a race of devils." The *locus classicus* of this confidence is the United States Constitution, whose famous system of checks and balances is an institutional antidote to office-holders who, if not quite a race of devils, are nevertheless a race with little public spirit and much private passion. In the words of Madison's famous formula in *Federalist #51*: "Ambition must be made to counteract ambition. The interest of the man must be connected with the constitutional rights of the place."

When Solzhenitsyn sadly remarks that in the West *"the letter of the law . . . is considered to be the supreme solution"* to conflict, and that *"everybody operates at the extreme limit of the legal frames,"* his objection goes to the root of the modern outlook, and to the heart of America's constitutional arrangements. The reliance on institutions instead of the formation of character—the commitment to a "policy of supplying, by opposite and rival interests, the defect of better motives," in Madison's phrase— appears to Solzhenitsyn mean and deficient. *"I have spent all my life under a Communist regime and I will tell you that a society without any objective legal scale is a terrible one indeed,"* he says. *"But a society with no other scale but the legal one is not quite worthy of man either."*

The alternative to reliance on institutions and the letter of the law is not tyranny or Czarist authoritarianism or the absence of law, but *"voluntary self-restraint."* This means moral education of the sort that teaches reason to rule the passions; moral education of the sort taught by Plato, Aristotle, Augustine, and others. As moral virtue is important in an individual, so good character is important in a people; and the role of law is to help shape a people's character. The modern reliance on institutions, commerce, and other substitutes for virtue implies a separation of law and morality where once there was merely a distinction. It is this separation that has provided *"access for evil."* Though the *"tilt of freedom in the direction of evil has come about gradually . . . it was evidently born primarily out of a humanistic and benevolent concept according to which there is no evil inherent in human nature; the world belongs to mankind and all the defects of life are caused by wrong social systems which must be corrected."*

In the modern view, *"everything beyond physical well-being and accumulation of material goods, all other human requirements and characteristics of a subtler and higher nature, [are] left outside the range of attention of the state and the social system."* Government, according to the familiar metaphor, is an umpire, seeing only that the most elementary and necessary rules are obeyed; scant attention is paid to the quality of the players as men; little effort is expended to educate them in virtue. The result is *"an atmosphere of moral mediocrity, paralyzing man's noblest impulses."*

The present peril of the West, its weakness and uncertainty, may therefore be traced to *"the very basis of human thinking in the past centuries,"* what Solzhenitsyn calls *"rationalistic humanism or humanistic autonomy: the proclaimed and enforced autonomy of man from any higher force above him."* Modernity, to put it simply, has been a mistake, a grave intellectual error. *"We are now experiencing the consequences of mistakes which had not been noticed at the beginning of the journey,"* he observes, hauntingly. *"On the way from the Renaissance to our days we have enriched our experience, but we have lost the concept of a Supreme Complete Entity which used to restrain our passions and our irresponsibility."* This loss—of the idea of God, or of nature, in the classical understanding—is the *"real crisis"* of our time, for *"the split in the world is less terrible than the fact that the same disease plagues its two main sections."*

A New Height of Vision

Modernity, in short, is in many ways a greater danger to man than Communism, which is only a particularly pathological mode of modernity—the marriage of the worst of modern science (and philosophy) with tyranny. Conservatives who are used to acclaiming Solzhenitsyn should understand that he is not merely anti-Communist but *anti-modern*, which means anti-capitalist as well.

He objects to Machiavelli, Hobbes, Locke, Madison, and Adam Smith as well as to Marx, though of course not so *much* as he objects to Marx.

Solzhenitsyn's opposition to modernity should not be identified as an opposition to the West. He is, in many ways, the greatest living representative of the West, an avatar of the West's most ancient and honorable principles. It is, for instance, no exaggeration to say that his understanding of man and politics is more intelligible in the context of the *Nicomachean Ethics* than of *War and Peace,* though that is not to gainsay his fierce love of the Russian people and their culture. But, on the one hand, having witnessed the diminution of man by modern science, and, on the other, having known that greatness of which the human soul is capable even in the most terrible circumstances, it's not surprising that he should reappraise, indeed resurrect, the almost forgotten alternative to modernity: classical and early Christian political philosophy.

He admitted as much at Harvard. *"It is imperative to review the table of widespread human values,"* he exhorted. *"Its present incorrectness is astounding. . . . We cannot avoid revising the fundamental definitions of human life and human society"* if man wishes to *"save life from self-destruction."* Whither shall man turn to recover the idea of a *"Supreme Complete Entity"*? Not to the *"Modern Era,"* not even to its early expressions. Nor to the Middle Ages, which reached their *"natural end"* in an *"intolerable despotic repression of man's physical nature in favor of the spiritual one."* Here at last is the final meaning of the title "A World Split Apart." For as between the Middle Ages and the Modern Era the human world is, so to speak, split apart. *"We shall have a rise to a new height of vision, to a new level of life where our physical nature will not be cursed as in the Middle Ages, but, even more importantly, our spiritual being will not be trampled upon as in the Modern Era."* The union of the sundered human world, of man as soul and body, would thus seem to belong to the one period of Western history he does not mention—those many centuries of classical thought stretching back beyond the Middle Ages.

When Solzhenitsyn declared that the contemporary West could

not serve as a proper model for his country, he touched the love-it-or-leave-it nerve of many Americans. Yet he emphasized, on that unforgettable Thursday afternoon in Cambridge, that the bitterness he spoke was the bitterness of truth, that it had come *"not from an adversary but from a friend."* "Enemies never tell men the truth," Tocqueville wrote. "Just because I am a friend do I dare to say these things [about democracy]." Solzhenitsyn's address at Harvard struck this senior as a reminder of what I see the West as having lost, and what it must regain, if it is to survive *"the trials of our time"*; his message was part warning, part prophecy, but also part encouragement. Though the *"moral heritage of Christian centuries"* has been attenuated, natural right and natural law neglected, voluntary self-restraint abjured— still, Western man may have time to learn again the lessons of self-government. If Solzhenitsyn is more insistent about those lessons than the politic Tocqueville, that is because *"the forces of Evil have begun their decisive offensive."* And time, for the West, is running out.

ARCHIBALD MACLEISH

Our Will Endures

EVER SINCE TOM PAINE, the American people have had the counsel and advice of friends from abroad in the long American debate about the purpose of the Republic. Was our Revolution, as Jefferson believed to his life's end, a "signal of arousing men to burst the chains," or was it simply a War of Independence, as John Adams kept saying? Tom Paine was on Jefferson's side in that. Was it "the Union" we were struggling to preserve, as Webster thought, in the years before the Civil War, or was Mr. Lincoln right at Gettysburg? Scores of English writers told us what to think about that issue. And now that we are a great power, leader of the free world in its confrontation with the most powerful and repressive police state in modern history, the debate goes on and the counsel and advice go with it. Are we responsible for the revolution of mankind which our Revolution launched? Solzhenitsyn spoke to us of that at Harvard at a great commencement under crimson banners in the June rain.

Solzhenitsyn is one of the most admirable men alive—a fine novelist, which means a trained and disciplined observer of the realities of human life—a man of noble spirit and unrivaled courage—a truly heroic figure who has suffered something close to martyrdom for his convictions. But Solzhenitsyn, unlike many of his predecessors in earlier generations, knows little of our American lives or of ourselves. His concern, understandably, is with his native country in its agony. He is an exile from the state police, an exile of the human spirit.

ARCHIBALD MACLEISH *is a poet and the author of many books. This article appeared in "Time," June 26, 1978, and is reprinted by permission (© 1978 by Time Incorporated).*

And he judges the Republic as such an exile would. Are we prepared, he asks, to oppose the tyranny which now rules Holy Russia and all the East of Europe? Are we prepared to risk our lives in such a struggle? Have we the courage? Or are we so softened by our generation of affluence, by our secular indifference to the human spirit, that we dare not fight? But though he asks these daring questions here—at Harvard—in a village in Vermont where he now lives—he is not truly *here* to ask them. He sees few Americans, speaks little English, and what he knows of the Republic he knows not from human witnesses but from television programs, which present their depressing parody of American life to him as they present it also to us but with this difference—that we know the parody for what it is.

He reproves us for faults which would not be faults if he could talk to his neighbors in Vermont, to his fellow writers, his fellow men. We are irresponsible, he tells us. We put our freedom first, before our responsibility. But if he could talk to us, he would realize that we put our freedom first before our responsibility because we are a free people—because a free people is a people that rules itself—because it must decide for itself what its responsibilities are—because there is no one else to decide this for us—neither the state police nor a state church nor anyone.

If he could talk to us—if he had talked to us—he would know that we are not irresponsible, that we establish our responsibilities for ourselves, seriously, painfully often.

And the same thing is true of our national will, which Solzhenitsyn talked to us about at Harvard on that June day in the cool rain. We have lost it, he told us, as though he had questioned us and knew our minds. But he had not questioned us and he did not know our minds. It is less than 40 years since the Second World War faced us with an issue which would have torn us apart had we not been free and so answerable to ourselves and to each other. We resolved that issue. We reached an agreement with each other about what we had to do. We did it. We reached the highest point in our history. And we have not changed. We have not changed in that one generation and will not change in another or another.

If Solzhenitsyn had talked to us—to a few of his neighbors in that village in Vermont—three or four of those who respect and admire him throughout the country—he would not have spoken those sentences at Harvard. He would have learned that we know who we are and what we have to become. He would have learned that we have not lost our will as a people—that it is precisely our will as a people which makes us true believers in that human spirit for which he means to speak.

MARY MCGRORY

Solzhenitsyn Doesn't Love Us

ALEXANDER SOLZHENITSYN'S HARVARD commencement speech has occasioned a good deal of grumbling.

Its immediate audience, the graduates, can hardly have gone forth from the Yard with light steps and the feeling of new worlds to conquer. The bearded prophet dispensed with the usual amenities and clichés that are handed out with diplomas. The class of 1978 heard nothing to cheer about—they are unindicted co-conspirators in the decline of the West.

It did not, of course, come as a surprise that Solzhenitsyn believes we should have persevered in Viet Nam. He is a dissenter who did not appreciate our dissent. He would fight the Communists on every front.

He despises our press. One of the reasons he deplores it is that it publishes "secret matters pertaining to one's national defense." It came as no shock that he regards us as "hasty, immature, superficial, and misleading." At any one time, all of the above are true about part of our trade.

But to have a man who is perhaps the century's most gifted and celebrated victim of the state defending state secrecy is, well, a disappointment.

So is having him advocating a form of government that sounds czarist. He didn't exactly come out and declare for a return to the

MARY MCGRORY *is a writer for the "Washington Star" whose column is carried by the Universal Press Syndicate. This article appeared in June 1978 and is reprinted by permission of the Washington Star Syndicate.*

good old days, but it was implicit in what he said about the West's trammeled statesmen, surrounded by "thousands of irresponsible critics" and "parliament and the press rebuffing him."

The czars, good or bad, did not have those particular problems, and Solzhenitsyn declares that "the restrictions imposed by democracy" have contributed to the "triumph of mediocrity."

"An outstanding and particularly gifted person," one like himself, for instance, might get a better hearing in an imperial Russia.

But nothing Solzhenitsyn said went so much against the grain as his negative view of our society. The unspoken expectation was that after three years in our midst, he would have to say we are superior, that our way is not only better, but best.

Compared to the Gulag Archipelago, Cavendish, Vt., has to be heaven on earth. We were, whether we admit it or not, waiting to hear him say it. He did not. Could the man who fought for his personal freedom with a valor and persistence, and chronicled the struggle in literary masterworks, at least have given one cheer for the extension of freedom to a whole society, even if it means some of the uglinesses he mentioned like "intolerable music" and pornography.

It is hard for us to face the fact that the giant does not love us, that he finds us hasty, shallow, overdosing on facts, but deficient in judgment and spirituality.

Maybe we would be better off if we stopped grappling with the politics and even the morality of what Solzhenitsyn said at Harvard and look at it in a different way—as the personal statement of a conservative, religious, and terribly homesick Russian.

We should never have expected the facile tributes which our immigrants—and our politicians—are forever paying us. Solzhenitsyn is not an immigrant, as he reminded us. He is an exile.

He is a Russian, and Russians are the world's supreme sufferers. The United States has no comparable cult of suffering—unless you count the joggers, who are simply seeking what Solzhenitsyn deplores as much as anything, the well-being which destroys the soul.

He could not miss the daily horrors of life in Moscow. But he misses those ridiculously brave people who were his comrades in the unequal battle against the monster-state. He has met no one here who compares with them:

"A fact which cannot be disputed is the weakening of human beings in the West while in the East they are becoming firmer and stronger. . . . We have been through a spiritual training far in advance of Western experience. Life's complexity and mortal weight have produced stronger, deeper, and more interesting characters than those generated by standardized Western well-being."

This is a theme you hear from other Soviet dissidents. They long for the homeland. Life in Moscow for a dissident is ghastly, but it is heady. Life has purpose and an edge. The sense of unity, which some people only experience on night patrols, picket lines, or death vigils, is overwhelming and constant. Yes, they might be clapped off to a mental hospital or a forced labor camp in the next instant, but while they are free, they can call once a week on one of the world's noblest men, Andrei Sakharov. They are, while their breath lasts, wholly alive.

Like Solzhenitsyn, they are often let down when they see what freedom is really like, with its multiple choices, its competitiveness, its near chaos. It is only human, as we know from our reaction to his Harvard speech, to expect more.

ARTHUR SCHLESINGER, JR.

The Solzhenitsyn
We Refuse to See

Wherefore is all this evil come upon us? Is it not because we have forsaken the Lord? . . . Do not our follies and iniquities testify against us? Have we not, especially in our Seaports, gone much too far into the pride and luxuries of life? Is it not a fact open to common observation, that profaneness, intemperance, unchastity, the love of pleasure, fraud, avarice, and other vices, are increasing among us from year to year? . . . Have our Statesmen always acted with integrity?

SAMUEL LANGDON, PRESIDENT OF HARVARD, 1775

THE VOICE THAT ECHOED in Harvard Yard on June 8 would not have surprised the first several generations of Harvard men. For Alexander Solzhenitsyn renewed an ancient and, in those precincts, forgotten tradition of apocalyptic prophecy. Not only looking but sounding like a figure from the Old Testament, he preached an impassioned sermon, warning America of the progress of evil and the imminence of judgment, urging Americans to repent their sins, forsake their idols and prostrate themselves before the "Supreme Complete Deity."

Few men living have as clearly earned the right to assume the prophetic stance. Solzhenitsyn is a man of exemplary nobility and

ARTHUR SCHLESINGER, JR., *is professor of humanities at the City University of New York and the author of more than a dozen books. This article appeared in the "Washington Post," June 25, 1978, and is reprinted by permission.*

extreme bravery. A powerful novelist and an indispensable historian, he is an artist and moralist who has taken unto himself the suffering of his countrymen and has magnificently indicted a vile regime in the name of the Soviet peoples and of Russian history. When Solzhenitsyn speaks, the world has a duty to listen. But it must listen with care, understanding that prophecy has its own dogma and that prophets are not infallible. "The prophesying business," as Mencken said, "is like writing fugues; it is fatal to everyone save the man of absolute genius."

Solzhenitsyn's Harvard speech, like much prophetic utterance, lacks clear development of argument. Casual readers, instead of trying to disentangle the threads of his discourse, have seized upon his more sensational judgments, such as his assertion that "a decline in courage" is "the most striking feature which an outside observer notices in the West." This decline, he continued, is "particularly noticeable among the ruling groups and the intellectual elite." It has led to a foreign policy founded on "weakness and cowardice." The American refusal to win the war in Vietnam, Solzhenitsyn declares, is a grievous and perhaps decisive example of the "loss of willpower in the West."

He finds the United States equally a failure at home. The "boundless space" granted "destructive and irresponsible freedom" has resulted, Solzhenitsyn tells us, in an "abyss of human decadence," marked by the "revolting invasion of publicity, by TV stupor, and by intolerable music," by pornography, crime, and horror. The pervading legalism of American society has become a shoddy substitute for internal self-discipline.

Most dangerous of all, in his view, is the unconstrained freedom permitted the press. The mass media are corrupt and licentious, unwilling to confess or correct error, inundating the people with "superficial and misleading judgments" and an "excessive burdening flow of information." Yet "the press has become the greatest power within the western countries." "By what law has it been elected," Solzhenitsyn asks, "and to whom is it responsible?"

It is easy but pointless to note that Solzhenitsyn sounds rather like Gen. LeMay on Vietnam, like Pravda on American pornography and like Spiro T. Agnew on the American press. Certainly these and other items in his bill have struck responsive chords in many American breasts. But his specific charges cannot be easily divorced from his cosmic philosophy. One wonders how many who applaud his Harvard speech realize what a blanket endorsement of Solzhenitsyn implies.

Perhaps more people applaud Solzhenitsyn than read him. His Harvard jeremiad implied a broad set of judgments. The West went wrong, he believes, with the Renaissance and the 18th century Enlightenment. "We turned our backs upon the Spirit and embraced all that is material with excessive and unwarranted zeal."

Communism is an abomination, but so is capitalism. Commercial interest tended to "suffocate" spiritual life. Or, as he put it in 1973, "no incentive to self-limitation ever existed in bourgeois economics. . . . It was a reply to the shamelessness of unlimited money-grubbing that socialism in all its forms developed." For all their differences, communism and capitalism are equally the end-products of "the logic of materialistic development."

Just as Solzhenitsyn's conservative admirers will reject his views on capitalism, so his liberal admirers will reject his views on democracy—views his great fellow-dissident, Andrei Sakharov, characterized in 1975 as "untrue and disturbing." Sakharov, for example, wants to liberalize and democratize the Soviet Union. He calls for a multi-party system and for the establishment of civil liberties. Little could be more remote from Solzhenitsyn's intentions. In 1975 he dismissed the Sakharov program as one more example of Russia's "traditional passive imitation of the West."

"A society in which political parties are active," he said, "never rises in the moral scale. . . . Are there no *extraparty* or *nonparty* paths of national development?" As for civil liberty, "the West," he wrote in 1969, "has supped more than its fill of every kind of freedom, including intellectual freedom. And has this saved it? We see it today crawling on hands and knees, its will paralyzed." (This was five years before he went into exile. His Harvard testimony therefore recorded not what he discovered after he came west but what he had always believed about the West.)

To regard freedom "as the object of our existence," he said in

1973, "is nonsense. . . . There is, therefore, a miscalculation in the urgent pursuit of political freedom as the first and main thing." He finds it equally nonsensical to regard earthly happiness as the object of existence. At Harvard he expressly rejected the proposition that "man lives to be free and to pursue happiness. (See, for example, the American Declaration of Independence.)"

In short, Solzhenitsyn has no belief in what he called at Harvard "the way of western pluralistic democracy." People lived for centuries without democracy, he wrote in 1973, "and were not always worse off." Russia under authoritarian rule "did not experience episodes of self-destruction like those of the 20th century, and for 10 centuries millions of our peasant forebears died feeling that their lives had not been too unbearable." In "patriarchal" societies people "even experienced that 'happiness' we are forever hearing about." Moreover, they preserved the health of the nation—"a level of moral health incomparably higher than that expressed today in simian radio music, pop songs and insulting advertisements." Undermined by the cult of freedom, he said at Harvard, "administrative power has been drastically reduced in all western countries."

As against democracy, with its weakness, mediocrity and moral chaos, Solzhenitsyn prefers systems "based on subordination to authority."

His objection to the Soviet system, he has explained, is "not because it is undemocratic, authoritarian, based on physical constraint—a man can live in such conditions without harm to his spiritual essence." His objection is that "over and above its physical constraints, it demands of us total surrender of our souls." Authoritarian regimes "*as such* are not frightening—only those which are answerable to no one and nothing." The autocrats of religious ages "felt themselves responsible before God. . . . The autocrats of our own time are dangerous precisely because it is difficult to find higher values which would bind them."

Solzhenitsyn's ideal has nothing to do with liberal democracy. If asked whether he saw the West "as a model to my country, frankly I would have to answer negatively." His ideal is a Christian authoritarianism governed by God-fearing despots without benefit of politics, parties, undue intellectual freedom or undue concern for popular happiness. Repression, indeed, is good for the soul. "The need to struggle against our surroundings," he wrote in 1973, "rewards our efforts with greater inner success."

Even today the Soviet Union, he assures us, provides a healthier moral environment than the United States. "Through intense suffering our country has now achieved a spiritual development of such intensity," he said at Harvard, "that the western system in its present state of spiritual exhaustion does not look attractive." The superior moral weight and complexity of life in the U.S.S.R. produce "stronger, deeper and more interesting characters than those generated by standardized Western well-being." Where the Declaration of Independence talked about life, liberty and the pursuit of happiness, Solzhenitsyn's essential thesis is strength through suffering.

For Solzhenitsyn, with his organic view of society, the nation even more than the individual is the crucial moral unit. Nations too can partake of the mystique of suffering. They "are very vital formations, susceptible to all moral feelings, including—however painful a step it may be—repentance." In his fascinating essay, "Repentance and Self-Limitation in the Life of Nations," published in 1975, Solzhenitsyn argued that "repentance is now a matter of life and death," for the sake not merely of life beyond the grave but of "our very survival on this earth."

Repentance, he tells us, will lead nations on to the possibility of self-limitation. "Such a change will not be easy for the free economy of the West. It is a revolutionary demolition and total reconstruction of all our ideas and aims. . . . We must abjure the plague of expansion beyond our borders, the continuous scramble after new markets and sources of raw material, increases in our industrial territory or the volume of production, the whole insane pursuit of wealth, fame and change."

He condemns equally the foreign policy of his own country: "We are ready in our conceit to extend our responsibility to any other country, however distant. . . . We meddle indefatigably in conflicts on every continent, lay down the law, shove people into quarrels, shamelessly push arms till they have become our most important item of export."

All this, he said, is catastrophically wrong. "Let us give up trying to restore order overseas, keep our grabbing imperial hands off neighbors who want to live their own lives. . . . We must stop running out into the street to join every brawl and instead retire virtuously into our own homes so long as we are in such a state of disorder and confusion." The nation must concentrate on its *inner* tasks: on healing its soul, educating its children, putting its own house in order. "Should we be struggling for warm seas far away, or ensuring that warmth rather than enmity flows between our citizens?"

These eloquent words might have come from speeches by George Kennan or George McGovern. Yet, when Americans repenting the excesses of Vietnam call for a policy of self-limitation, Solzhenitsyn, instead of rejoicing in converts, denounces them as cowards. Can he really believe that bombing the Vietnamese back to the Stone Age is a test of courage?

Still, prophets are not always consistent. Perhaps, as a fervent Russian nationalist, he is more concerned with the salvation of Russia than of America. He should not be so contemptuous of Americans, who want to save their own souls. Or perhaps his is the understandable frustration of the messenger who tries to tell the West about the true nature of Soviet tyranny and encounters only blandness and complacency.

Before the Second World War Arthur Koestler wrote with comparable frustration about the inability of the victims of Nazism to make the British believe their personal testimony about Hitler's terror. Later Koestler decided that what the English lacked was not courage but imagination. No doubt it was this very lack of imagination that made Britain stand alone against Hitler after the fall of France. Maybe Solzhenitsyn understands the United States as little as Koestler understood the Britain of 1939.

In any event, Solzhenitsyn at Harvard was offering only fragments of a grand vision of the nature and destiny of man. Regeneration can come, for nations as well as for individuals, only through confession of sin and acknowledgement of the sovereignty of the Almighty. This vision would have been familiar to the Puritan divines who preached in Harvard Yard three centuries ago. It includes the premonitions of Armageddon, the final struggle with Satan. "The forces of Evil have begun their decisive offensive," Solzhenitsyn cried at Harvard. "You can feel their pressure." It partakes of the millennial dream as set forth in the books of Daniel and of Revelation. "If the world has not come to its end, it has approached a major turn in history. . . . it will exact from us a spiritual upsurge."

This is a great, searching vision. In its majesty and profundity, in its perception of the evil inherent in human nature, it exposes the shallow religiosity of a born-again White House that, against every Augustinian and Calvinist insight, proclaims the doctrine of the inherent goodness of man and the aspiration to produce a government as good, decent, virtuous, loving, etc., as the American people. The challenge to American smugness and hedonism, to the mediocrity of our mass culture, to the decline of self-discipline and civic spirit, is bracing and valuable.

To this extent Solzhenitsyn shares common ground with our Puritan ancestors. But Solzhenitsyn's faith is suffused, in addition, by the other-worldly mysticism of the Russian Church—a mysticism that reflected the political absolutism of Russian society. By Russian religious standards, earthly happiness is nothing compared to the divine judgment.

The Puritan tradition was more empirical. Even the New England ministry had to temper its conviction of divine sovereignty with concession to the rough democracy of a nonprescriptive society, where men made their way in life through their own labor. In the 18th century Calvinism absorbed John Locke and laid the philosophical basis for the American experiment in democracy.

This is why the two traditions diverged—why the Solzhenitsyn vision, with its fear of human freedom, its indifference to human happiness, its scorn for democracy, its faith in the authoritarian state, is so alien to the great tradition of the West. The greatest American theologian of our own time, Reinhold Niebuhr, demolished years ago the mystical illusion that nations have souls like individuals. Nor would he for a moment accept the authoritarian pretense that rulers, when avowing religious faith, are thereby rendered more immune than the rest of us to the corruptions of power. "The worst corruption," said Niebuhr, "is a corrupt religion"; and of course, "Man's capacity for justice makes democracy possible, but man's inclination toward injustice makes democracy necessary."

At Harvard Solzhenitsyn remarked that the West "never understood" Russia. One may respond that Solzhenitsyn has never understood America. He arrived complete with preconceptions about American decadence and cowardice and evidently nothing he has found in the mass media has disabused him. But, as Archibald MacLeish has well said, "What he knows of the Republic he knows not from human witnesses but from television programs, which present their depressing parody of American life to him as they present it also to us, but with this difference—that we know the parody for what it is."

He comes, moreover, as a messenger of God. "Truth eludes us," he said at Harvard, "if we do not concentrate with total attention on its pursuit." He has concentrated with total attention and does not doubt that the truth is his.

But the notion of absolute truth is hard for Americans to take. If absolute truth exists, it is certainly not something confided intact to frail and sinful mortals. Mr. Dooley long ago defined fanatics as men who do what they think "th' Lord wud do if He only knew the facts in th' case." And Jefferson in his first inaugural: "Sometimes it is said that man cannot be trusted with the government of himself. Can he, then be trusted with the government of others? Or have we found angels in the form of kings to govern him? Let history answer this question." History has answered this question with terrible certitude in the 20th century. "The unfortunate thing," Pascal said long before, "is that he who would act the angel acts the brute."

If prophecy is one Christian virtue, humility is another. Knowing the crimes committed in the name of a single Truth, Americans prefer to keep their ears open to a multitude of competing lower-case truths. Ours has been a nation of skepticism, experiments, accommodation, self-criticism, piecemeal but constant reform—a mixture of traits repugnant to the authoritarian and messianic personality, but perhaps not too bad for all that.

Americans were deemed as sinful in 1678 as Solzhenitsyn

deems them in 1978; the Day of Judgment was quite as near and remote then as now. We welcome his presence and honor his witness; but he must understand the irrelevance of his grand vision to a democratic and libertarian society. Emerson, as usual, said it best:

> *I like the church, I like a cowl,*
> *I love a prophet of the soul;*
> *And on my heart monastic aisles*
> *Fall like sweet strains or pensive smiles;*
> *Yet not for all his faith can see*
> *Would I that cowled churchman be.*

PART THREE
LATER REFLECTIONS

RONALD BERMAN

Through Western Eyes

Or, at one bound o'er-leaping all his laws,
Make God Man's Image, Man the final Cause,
Find Virtue local, all relation scorn,
See all in Self, and but for self be born.

ALEXANDER POPE, *THE DUNCIAD*

SOLZHENITSYN POSES A PROBLEM different from that of most men of letters who comment on public affairs. Wordsworth lived long enough to repent his views on the French Revolution; Shaw, Yeats, and Pound retained their reputations despite their political beliefs. Very few artists or novelists have managed to affect the world *because* of their political beliefs. Solzhenitsyn has insisted on making his ideas of culture and politics central to his work—in fact, they are the work itself.

Solzhenitsyn is not a great novelist. He is good, better than nearly all his contemporaries, but not in the first rank of world literature. We respond to his art because he is a great man, on the scale of many a martyr or saint. His fiction matters to us because it is historically persuasive, because it seems *true*. Few critics in the free world would challenge his accuracy in depicting the Communist world, whether in his novels or in *The Gulag Archipelago*. His great strength is understanding and depiction. His work has a unique ability to portray the relation between the individual and the state. He has—or had until the appearance of this speech—convinced us that he understands the ideas, expec-

---

RONALD BERMAN *is professor of Renaissance literature at the University of California, San Diego. He formerly was chairman of the National Endowment for the Humanities. His books include "America in the Sixties: An Intellectual History."*

tations, and morals that are our cultural battleground.

"A World Split Apart" matters for its analysis of Western thought, not for its observations on Western institutions. Solzhenitsyn is wrong about the operation of the press in the West, for example. He has confused the idea of legalism with the nature of the legal system. And he has suggested that intellectual life is shaped by the media—although the press generally reflects the incoming and outgoing tides of the intellectual community. Yet though he may be unfamiliar with the operation of these institutions, he is on firm ground when he considers their cultural context. In addressing specific ideas of the West he is at a disadvantage; but his overall analysis of Western ideas cannot be easily dismissed.

A large and increasingly significant segment of modern scholarship sees in the Enlightenment pretty much what Solzhenitsyn describes in "A World Split Apart." We date from *part* of that eighteenth-century movement our rather shallow optimism about human nature and historical progress. And from the Enlightenment also proceeds our exaggerated confidence in the powers of both reason and government. Solzhenitsyn's intellectual sources are somewhat older; they go back, as George Will suggests, to St. Augustine. A notable passage in "A World Split Apart" deals with the idea of freedom:

> In early democracies, as in American democracy at the time of its birth, . . . freedom was given to the individual conditionally, on the assumption of his constant religious responsibility. Such was the heritage of the preceding millennium. Two hundred— or even fifty—years ago, it would have seemed quite impossible, in America, for an individual to be granted unrestrained freedom simply for the indulgence of his passions. . . . The West has finally upheld the rights of man, even to excess. But man's sense of responsibility to God and society has faded away.

As a view of the intentions of America's Founding Fathers, this passage seems unexceptionable: it distills many of the convictions of *The Federalist Papers*. As a historical description it seems accurate: freedom is a Christian rather than a classical idea, depending on the belief in universal human value, even of slaves. As a psychological insight, too, the passage seems right: freedom can never be absolute and will always be affected by the principle of diminishing returns. It is sobering to compare Solzhenitsyn on freedom with what Hannah Arendt says in *The Human Condition.* Consider the following lines from that great work:

> The trouble with modern theories of behaviorism is not that they are wrong but that they could become true, that they actually are the best possible conceptualization of certain obvious trends in modern society. It is quite conceivable that the modern age—which began with such an unprecedented and promising outburst of human activity—may end in the deadliest, most sterile passivity history has ever known. . . . Man may be willing and, indeed, is on the point of developing into that animal species from which, since Darwin, he imagined he has come [Doubleday, 1959, p. 295].

Both the Solzhenitsyn and the Arendt passages are based upon the conviction that secular society rests upon values it has not itself provided, and that it may be less than it ought to be because it demands less than it should of itself.

In other passages Solzhenitsyn discusses the deficiencies common to all post-Enlightenment thought, with its shallow view of behavior, morals, and social responsibility. The *New York Times* evidently refers to this part of the speech when it detects a conflict between enlightened and enthusiastic (i.e., fanatic) points of view. I believe the *Times* was wrong about this. I take Solzhenitsyn to mean that the *intentions* of Enlightenment ideas are not enough in human affairs. If human affairs are complex and sometimes irrational, then it can do no good to impose mechanistic, materialistic, or rationalistic solutions on them, to assume that behavior can be modified, character changed, and perceptions altered.

The *Times* also suggests that the speech is about the opposition of God and the Devil; I hope its editors are never turned loose on *Paradise Lost.* That epic is about making sense of human history. And Solzhenitsyn's speech, in a more direct way, is about the same thing. There is indeed a conflict, but it is between different kinds of social analysis. The author of "A World Split Apart" is like those who, having read Burke, Kierkegaard, and Freud, have a healthy suspicion of human reason, and who do not foresee the end of discontents in civilization. It may well be that Solzhenitsyn is devoutly (even hopelessly) Russian Orthodox. But that set of beliefs does not supply the essence of his argument. The Harvard speech is not an apology for a religious commonwealth. It is an affirmation that human nature is best understood through religious concepts. By suggesting human and social irrationality, Solzhenitsyn is not simplifying. He brings a complex analysis to a complex subject.

The most important single thing that can be said of "A World Split Apart" is that it is *a reading of the West through Western eyes*. The early commentators had one reaction in common: they found the speech to be different from their expectations. Having done so, they were ready to think that it was outside their experience and traditions. But to read the speech in scholarly tranquility is to be aware of its intellectual familiarity. Any basic library of Western thought will contain its ideas; dozens of writers from St. Augustine on would find in it some of their own thoughts. To take one example: Dr. Johnson's essays in the *Rambler, Idler,* and *Adventurer* are full of Solzhenitsyn's moral concerns; and it is he who observes that to act independent of a moral foundation is to compound several kinds of nonsense: human happiness has to have some purpose, for if it were only an end, then *anything* producing it would be justifiable.

The responses to "A World Split Apart" were critical of its attitude toward the media and the law, and of its assertive morality in dealing with culture. Assertions like the following were found objectionable:

The laws are best explained, interpreted, and applied by those whose interest and abilities lie in perverting, confounding, and eluding them.

I see a press more mean, and paltry, and silly, and disgraceful than any country I ever knew.

Religion says: *the Kingdom of God is within you;* and culture, in like manner, places human perfection in an *internal* condition, in the growth and predominance of our humanity proper, as distinguished from our animality.

These passages, though close in spirit to parts of the Harvard speech to which critics took exception, were not written by Solzhenitsyn. The first is by Jonathan Swift; it is the conclusion of the King of Brobdingnag when the ways of the West are explained to him in *Gulliver's Travels*. Most readers would agree that the king is a moral norm in that book, and that his opinion is intended to convey the author's own. The second judgment is that of Charles Dickens, writing after an American lecture tour in which he was much offended by reporters and newspapers. The third passage is Matthew Arnold's. It comes from those essays in criticism that oppose "culture" and "anarchy" for the modern mind, and that have a good deal to do with our response to those ideas.

There are clearly good reasons to agree with those who have placed Solzhenitsyn in the tradition of Russian nationalist literature. He does address himself to the Russian character and society. His vision of the good society is Russia without Communism. But there is not much reason to interpret "A World Split Apart" as if it were wholly determined by nationality and religious faith. Like the rest of us, Solzhenitsyn seems to belong to more than one tradition. This is partly acknowledged whenever he is called "prophetic" and compared to the more absolute or puritanical moralists of the West—though the intention clearly is to date him and suggest that he belongs in the past. I have suggested that he participates in Western thought. That is, he is more than prophetic. He resembles, say, Swift and Burke in more than attitude, for he takes up ideas that they take up, and he argues in ways common among those thinkers who have established the anti-Enlightenment position. Here and elsewhere in his works Solzhenitsyn argues in a way familiar to the common reader. He is not optimistic about human nature or about government. He perceives human behavior to be more than somewhat irrational. He has no faith in materialism and has a qualified toleration of freedom. His vocabulary may be different, but there seems to be a strong resemblance between his sense of the materialistic and, say, Michael Oakeshott's definition of the rationalistic in political behavior. In short, readers from the conservative tradition will find that Solzhenitsyn consistently resembles the works that have framed their own imagination.

But the common reader will find even more. We recognize in "A World Split Apart" the literature of our own century. The speech reflects the ideas stated by Nietzsche, Conrad, Freud, Eliot, and those others whom we take to be the authors of the modern mind. It is not particularly the Slavophile movement but modernism that has shown us the great artistic themes of conflict within the human mind, hollowness in our social and political ideas, and the responsibility that has been thrust on every mind capable of consciousness.

Solzhenitsyn's attitude toward the West is not the pessimism of religious orthodoxy but the doubt expressed by Conrad about the effects of civilization when defined by purely political ideals. It contains the concerns of all writers aware that our society, brilliant and captivating and satisfying as it is, has faults that run too deep for it to endure. It is not enough, in analyzing Solzhenitsyn, to invoke the eccentricities of the Russian nineteenth century, or to compare what he says with the unguarded moments of Tolstoy and Dostoevsky. Among the Russian writers of the nineteenth century there were a good many who were enthusiastic about religion or philosophical ideas. We may feel compelled to compare life to life, but we must also compare work to work. Solzhenitsyn belongs with Lawrence and Freud, among others whose *secular* intuition brought them to conclusions that the crowd assembled in Harvard Yard might well have found equally uncomfortable.

Many a course in twentieth-century humanities will cover the points made by Solzhenitsyn in language very much like his. Such a course might well begin with the writings of T. E. Hulme, whose social and artistic philosophy was praised by Herbert Read and Jacob Epstein, and who influenced both Eliot and Pound. Hulme was much concerned with what both he and Solzhenitsyn have called "humanism." Solzhenitsyn believes that after the Renaissance, Western man became self-centered and materialistic; he stopped believing in evil and began to believe in his own essential

goodness and right to gratification. Few scholars will quarrel with
this conclusion—though there will be significant dissent about the
reasons for it. I would say that Solzhenitsyn has confused the
work of the humanists with later developments in ideas and behavior. The humanists of the Renaissance gave us a substantial
literature of moral values. Nevertheless, to compare Hulme's
Speculations with Solzhenitsyn's essay is to see highly compatible views of the cause and effect of certain Western problems.
Hulme, very much a part of modernism, argues that religion is
more than a moral necessity. He poses institutions against individuals casually liberated from them. And he has some very interesting passages about "personalities" that correspond to what
Solzhenitsyn says about character in a time of social crisis. Solzhenitsyn's charges of moral weakness and hedonism may result
not so much from personal crankiness as from an insight into what
Hulme called the "radical imperfection" of our personalities at
this particular stage in Western development. It is a subject taken
up with devastating effect by Christopher Lasch in his recent
book *The Culture of Narcissism.*

Solzhenitsyn writes not only about "stronger, deeper and more
interesting characters" that are being formed outside the West but
about the West's failure to produce civic leadership. In this his
views differ little from those of George Santayana in his landmark
book *The Winds of Doctrine.* The following could have been part
of "A World Split Apart":

> When chaos has penetrated so far into the moral being of na-
> tions they can hardly be expected to produce great men. A
> great man need not be virtuous, nor his opinions right, but he
> must have a firm mind, a distinctive, luminous character; if he is
> to dominate things, something must be dominant in him
> [Harper, 1957, p. 20].

Solzhenitsyn's comments on this point are headed not "Virtue"
but rather "Courage." I do not know whether he has read Santayana's essay "Modernism and Christianity," but those who
have can see the Harvard speech as far more representative than
idiosyncratic.

At the beginning of the present century, another novelist had a great deal to say about the motives of politics and the nature of society. In Conrad's fiction we find familiar themes: the inadequacy of ideals of perfection in *Heart of Darkness*; the "egocentric naïveties" (the phrase is from the noted British critic F. R. Leavis) of *The Secret Agent;* and skepticism about the unsupported virtues of human character in *Nostromo*. To call Solzhenitsyn "pessimistic" about human nature and human fate is to disregard the rather profound maturity of other "pessimists" of our own time.

A final example, one necessary in any study of the modern mind, is T. S. Eliot. In a superb essay called "Second Thoughts About Humanism," Eliot goes a long way to clarify ideas common to himself, to Solzhenitsyn, and to ourselves. It is Eliot, after all, who writes that "if I succeeded in proving that humanism is insufficient without religion, what is left for those who cannot believe?" Eliot is discussing the history, early in the twentieth century, of the movement called humanism, which may have developed from but is not identical to the humanism of the Renaissance. It is essentially a secular belief in the power of man to shape his own character and destiny. In response to the idea that religion is a matter of sensibility, ritual, or simply moral comfort, Eliot invokes Hulme's famous assertion: "It is not, then, that I put up with the dogma for the sake of the sentiment, but that I may possibly swallow the sentiment for the sake of the dogma." The dogma referred to is the accumulation of religious insight into the character of man and society. Hulme's point corresponds quite closely to those passages in "A World Split Apart" that take Western society to task for its *narrowness of imagination* rather than for its failure to conform to the author's preferences.

Much modern thought has been concerned with elaborating some meaning from the way we live. And from Eliot and Pound, who wrote about the deficient understanding of the secular imagination, to Irving Kristol, who has argued that because capitalism is materialistic it is unable to resist the attack made upon it by its own intellectuals, it has been widely recognized that the West has not expressed a moral imperative for its prosperity. In critically addressing the West, Solzhenitsyn is seeing it through Western eyes.

There are, then, two levels of discourse in this speech, and for the most part only one has engaged its critics. To identify Solzhenitsyn only with Russian Orthodoxy and its intellectual disabilities is to dismiss the likelihood that he participates in another tradition as well. He has been deeply affected by the same problems that have made so many of our Western thinkers hard for us to bear. It may be that we have confused the two kinds of criticism of the West. What "A World Split Apart" does is outline the preconditions of a genuinely free society. It is critical of the West but not mordant. In fact, it celebrates values that have made the West what it is. The heart of the speech is about the nature of freedom, the constraints on freedom—and the value of freedom. Its form and some of its incidental remarks brought it more criticism than its central message warrants. Perhaps Solzhenitsyn could have learned from Auden, who thought art should teach the free man how to praise. And perhaps his adversaries should have thought of Yeats, who warned us that an intellectual hatred is the worst.

SIDNEY HOOK

On Western Freedom

RARELY IN MODERN TIMES—especially in times of relative peace—has one man's voice provoked the Western world to an experience of profound soul-searching. What Aleksandr Solzhenitsyn said not only at Harvard in June 1978 but also earlier before the AFL-CIO (which provided him a platform when the President of the United States, at the urging of his Metternichian Secretary of State Henry Kissinger, refused to receive him) has stirred the reflective conscience of the Western world more profoundly than even the eloquent discourses of Franklin Roosevelt and Winston Churchill. This is all the more unprecedented because Solzhenitsyn speaks in a foreign tongue and uses expressions that remain opaque in translation. Nonetheless, the continuing comments on the Harvard speech testify to the power of his words and to the fundamental character of his challenge to our mode of life, to its basic values, fears, and illusions, and to a philosophy of civilization concealed by the apparent absence of any philosophy.

My response falls into four sections and then a final restatement of what I regard as Solzhenitsyn's morally valid challenge to the West despite the multitude of defects and inaccuracies in his analysis of the nature of freedom and democracy and the causes of the weakness of the West.

First I shall deal with his general indictment of the West. Sec-

SIDNEY HOOK *is senior research fellow at the Hoover Institution of War, Revolution and Peace, Stanford, California. He taught philosophy at New York University for more than forty years and is currently emeritus professor there. Among his books are "The Paradoxes of Freedom" and "The Ambiguous Legacy: Marx and the Marxists."*

ond, I shall consider some of his specifications of its decline and dangers. Third, I shall discuss his peculiar conception of democracy, his failure to appreciate the distinction between legality and morality, even granting the large measure of truth in his observation about the excesses of a freedom conceived only as the absence of restraint or the rejection of rational regulation. Fourth, I shall consider his causal analysis of our predicament, his central contention that all our evils can be attributed to the rise of secular, rational humanism and its belief that an acceptable human morality is intrinsically related to the consequences of our actions on human weal and woe. According to Solzhenitsyn, such a belief generates the heresy that morality is logically independent of religion and theology, especially of the existence of God as "the Supreme Complete Entity." Here Solzhenitsyn reveals not only his literary but also his spiritual kinship to his great countrymen, Dostoyevsky and Tolstoy.

Finally, after giving full measure to all of Solzhenitsyn's misunderstandings of Western culture, I should like to restate what I take to be his crucial, abiding, and valid messages to the partisans of human freedom in our time. On the basis of his central insight, I am confident that those who are opposed to *all* varieties of totalitarianism can work out a unifying moral program that is independent of all our theological and religious differences. Such an approach can serve as a common rallying point for those who still believe that in the current conflict between free and unfree societies, there are alternatives other than war and surrender. It makes possible a strategy for freedom that still holds out the promise not merely of survival but of a society worthy of human beings.

His Indictment of the West

The central point in Solzhenitsyn's indictment of the West is that it has suffered a colossal failure of nerve concerning its own animating philosophy of freedom, as expressed in its basic documentary ideals. According to him, the map of political freedom in the world is shrinking, and Western ideals are in eclipse even in those areas of the world that they helped to liberate. The vast gains in all forms of human freedom that have been made in social and political life are either denied or downgraded, in his eyes, by the continuing shortcomings that are apparent when we measure (as we should) the status quo against our highest standards.

In the Communist world, Solzhenitsyn charges, there is no genuine reciprocity either in cultural exchanges or in the honoring of pledges and agreements. The Helsinki Accords, in which the West formally acknowledged the de facto suzerainty of the Soviet Empire in Eastern Europe, have been violated by the failure of the Soviet Union and most of its satellites to live up to the elementary provisions of human rights to which they have pledged lip allegiance. The degrading treatment of the Scharanskys, the Ginsburgs, and the Grigorenkos, the enforced incarceration of dissidents in psychiatric torture chambers, continues. The Soviet Union's failure to uphold the Belgrade agreement to investigate the compliance with human rights brought no remonstrance from the United States.

In the so-called Third World, according to Solzhenitsyn, we have witnessed a strange transformation: colonially liberated countries whose ideals were related to, if not rooted in, the American Declaration of Independence are now ruled by one-party dictatorships whose treatment of the people equals or even surpasses in cruelty the oppression from which they were liberated. The United Nations has in effect become an association of anti-American nations more intent on transforming Israel, the victim of a systematic terror campaign, into a pariah state than on coping with the genocidal practices of Amin's Uganda or Cambodia.

But the main point in Solzhenitsyn's indictment of the Western world concerns its very conception of freedom. He believes the West is so obsessed with its notion of freedom that in exercising that freedom it cannot distinguish between what is desirable and what is undesirable to pursue. It defends individual *rights* to the point of making them almost absolute, refusing to understand that our essential freedoms cannot function properly unless we recognize that certain human *obligations* are just as binding upon us. "Legal limits (especially in the United States) are broad enough," he says, "to encourage not only individual freedom but also certain individual crimes. Supported by thousands of public defenders, criminals can remain unpunished or receive undeserved leniency. When a government seriously undertakes to fight terrorism, public opinion immediately accuses it of violating the terrorists' civil rights."

Many of Solzhenitsyn's formulations are inexact or exaggerated, but I think it is fair to restate his main philosophical points in the following assertions.

First, freedom is misconceived if it is defined as the right to do anything one pleases. Every specific freedom we can reasonably defend must be one that is desirable or normative.

Second, no desirable freedom can be unqualified; every right, whether moral or legal, carries with it a restriction or prohibition of the correlative right to interfere with it. If you sincerely believe that a person has a right to speak, write, assemble, and worship according to his conscience, then you must believe that no one has the right or freedom to prevent him from exercising this right, that the freedom to interfere with this right must be restrained. If you believe in tolerance, then you cannot believe in tolerating those who are *actively intolerant* of others. Otherwise you do not understand the meaning of tolerance or are insincere in professing belief in it.

Third, no matter what schedule of desirable rights or freedoms you draw up, none is absolute, because in every moral situation, rights conflict. In his own way Solzhenitsyn realizes what philosophers like John Dewey and others have expressed more precisely, that the moral situation confronts one with a conflict not between good and bad, right and wrong, but between the good and the good, and the right and the right. For instance, you cannot always give a man a right to a fair trial and permit complete freedom of the press. Kindness and truth are not always compatible. Lying is wrong, but so is murder—and sometimes you may have to choose between telling the truth and saving a life.

Legalism vs. Morality

But the biting impact of Solzhenitsyn's speeches lies not in his recognition of these truths but rather in his dramatic illustrations of what he regards as improper choices when values conflict. Two illustrations must suffice.

Of course Solzhenitsyn believes in freedom of the press—since he has been imprisoned and exiled because of its absence. But in the West he sees a press "more powerful than the legislature, the executive, and the judiciary," and a claim for its freedom regardless of the consequences for the nation's well-being and security. He asks: If everyone is to be held morally responsible and legally accountable in a just and democratic society, who holds the press responsible and accountable, especially if it enjoys a practical monopoly? He speaks of cases in which reporters steal government secrets and the press publishes them under the claim "the public has a right to know": when legal inquiries are made into the secret sources of a reporter's news, he says, even if a man's life or freedom is at stake, the press unanimously denies that the public has a right to know—on the grounds of freedom of the press. But if that is true, then may it not also be true that in the interests of preserving a free society—without which there could be no freedom of the press—the government may also claim that there are some secrets that the public does not, at least for a limited period, have a right to know?

A second illustration. Coming from a country in which people are often severely punished for living up to the laws of their own land, as the Soviet dissidents claim, Solzhenitsyn is taken aback by what he sees in this country as an excess of legalism over morality in the judicial system. This is related to what others have recently referred to as our imperial judiciary. At a time when there is a sharp incidence in major crimes of violence, he finds increasing concern with protecting the rights, not of the victims and potential victims of crime, but of those guilty or accused of crimes. He claims to find a jurisprudential theory according to which criminals are the victims of society and therefore not really responsible for their evil deeds; this results in the legally counte-

nanced resort to technical procedures and prolonged delays that
defeats the ends of justice. (If he had mentioned the absurdity of
the exclusionary rule in the area of evidence, he would have been
much more eloquent and morally indignant.) Rightly or wrongly
he associates these judicial conditions with the decline in private
and public morality, with an increase in selfishness, with the philosophy of grab-and-run-if-you-can. There is something wrong
with a society when "the center of your democracy and culture is
left for a few hours without electricity, just that, and instantly
crowds of American citizens rush to loot and rape."

The Press and American Democracy

Let us now turn to a more central point. Even if we grant the
validity of many of the *specific* criticisms in Solzhenitsyn's indictment (and in these matters of the law and abuses by the press
the picture seems to me to be very grim indeed), what does Solzhenitsyn suggest as a political cure or alternative? Here a fatal
ambiguity in his conception of democracy manifests itself, and I
shall relate this to his fundamental theology.

First of all, Solzhenitsyn fails to realize that many of the defects
in the current American legal process are not rooted in the democratic system. In democratic countries like England and Canada,
and even in some less democratic jurisdictions, without the
slightest abridgment of justice, the courts work much more effectively and the law is by far less egregiously an ass than in so many
of our state and federal jurisdictions.

This is even more obvious with respect to the press. Given the
present state of investigative reporting, the growth in some quar-
ters of advocacy reporting, and the view that because complete
objectivity is impossible, therefore the whole concept of objectivity is a myth, no man's or woman's reputation is safe from careless
and irresponsible misrepresentation. In this respect, professional
standards of media reporting in England are superior to those in
the United States, though even there they leave something to be
desired. Even without taking recourse to the English laws of libel
and the Official Secrets Act, one can repair to a Press Council if

one has been victimized by a false or malicious press story. But in the United States—

When the Twentieth Century Fund, on the advice of some leading figures in American journalism and based on the success of the British example, established a Press Council, such leading papers as *The New York Times* and *The Washington Post* refused to cooperate with that council. Indeed, the American Society of Newspaper Editors a few years ago voted three to one against the establishment of even its own internal grievance committee [Max Kampelman, "The Power of the Press," *Policy Review,* Fall 1978].

Lester Markel, a former editor of the *New York Sunday Times,* a few years ago wrote:

The press, pretending to believe that there is no credibility gap and asserting its near-infallibility, countenances no effective supervision of its operation; it has adopted a holier-than-thou attitude, citing the First Amendment and in addition the Ten Commandments and other less holy scripture [*New York Times,* February 2, 1973].

John B. Oakes, emeritus editorial-page editor of the *New York Times,* added his voice to the criticism of journalistic irresponsibility. In discussing the "Dwindling Faith in the Press" he pointed to the necessity of making the press "voluntarily more accountable as well as more accessible to the public" (*New York Times,* May 24, 1978). The more powerful it is, the more accountable it should be. Sometimes it abuses its power, as when by false reporting it transformed the military *disaster* suffered by the Viet Cong in its Tet Offensive into a military *victory.* The effect was to give a political victory to the Viet Cong in this country, force a President out of office, and profoundly affect the ultimate outcome of the war.

These are some of the evils of a democracy. But the cure, surely, is not *no* democracy but a *better* democracy. And there are ways and means of bettering a democracy without relying on the famous trinity of the Dostoyevskian tradition: mystery, authority, and miracles. What Solzhenitsyn fails to appreciate about Western democracy is the nature of its political faith. There is nothing sanctified about the will of a majority even when it recognizes the civil and human rights of its minorities. It is not infallible. The majority may be unenlightened, but as Felix Frankfurter put it, "the appeal from an unenlightened majority in a democracy is to an enlightened majority," and so long as the political process of registering freely given consent exists, the evils are remediable.

The real question we must ask Solzhenitsyn is whether he is prepared to accept the *risks* of a democracy and its right to be wrong, provided it has a chance to correct that wrong. Or does he believe, as do all totalitarians from Plato to those of the present, that most members of the community are either too stupid or too vicious to be entrusted with self-government? I, for one, believe that despite some ambiguous expressions, Solzhenitsyn, like his great compatriot Andrei Sakharov, can be counted on the side of democracy.

The fundamental argument for democracy against those who are convinced that they know the true interests of the people better than the people itself is: those who wear the shoes know best where they pinch and therefore have the right to change their political shoes in the light of their experience. Of course, children and mentally retarded persons do not always know when and where their shoes pinch. The totalitarians and their apologists justify their "paternalism"—which rests more on force and self-interest than on genuine concern for the people's welfare—by the arrogant assumption that the people are in a permanent state of childhood.

The West's Failure of Nerve

I come now to Solzhenitsyn's analysis of the causes of the failure of Western courage, the inadequacies of its democracy, and the weakness of its morality. And here I find him, together with a long line of distinguished predecessors and successors, profoundly, demonstrably, and tragically wrong. To Solzhenitsyn the cause of Western democratic decline and the collapse of its morality is the rise of secular humanism and rationalism, which began with the breakdown of the medieval synthesis and the emergence of the scientific world-outlook. Put in its simplest terms, what Solzhenitsyn is saying is that the basic cause of our world crisis is the erosion of religion, the decline in the belief in the existence of a Supreme Power or Entity, and our reliance not on transcendental faith but on human intelligence as a guide to man's nature and conduct.

I cannot accept Solzhenitsyn's causal analysis for many reasons. Historically, neither Judaism, Christianity, nor Islam is responsible for the emergence of democracy as a system of community self-government resting upon the freely given consent of the governed. None of these religions ever condemned slavery or feudalism in principle, and often they offered apologetic justifications for them. Logically, from the proposition that all men are equal in the sight of the Lord, it does not follow in the least that they are or should be equal in the sight of the Law. The belief in the divine right of kings is older than the equally foolish view *vox populi vox Dei*. The existence or non-existence of God is equally compatible with the existence of any social system whatsover, except when God is so defined that his moral attributes require that the system be democratic.

My criticism goes even further. Theology is irrelevant not only to democracy and capitalism and socialism as social systems but to the validity of morality itself. Solzhenitsyn echoes Smerdyakov's dictum in Dostoevsky's *Brothers Karamazov* that "if God does not exist, everything is [morally] permissible." But this is a non-sequitur. Men build their gods in their own moral image. When we profess to derive a moral command from a religious revelation, it is only because we have smuggled into our conception of Divinity our own moral judgments. By definition God cannot do evil, but we ourselves are responsible for the distinction between good and evil. What makes an action morally valid is not a command from on high or from anywhere else but the intrinsic character of the action and its consequences for human weal and woe.

Some of the profoundest theologians of the West, from the

author of the original version of the Book of Job to Augustine to Kierkegaard, have maintained that the religious dimension of human experience transcends the moral experience. The bone in the throat of Western theology is the problem of evil—the ever-recurrent question why an allegedly all-powerful and all-benevolent Supreme Being permits in every age the torture of innocent multitudes. Kierkegaard in his *Fear and Trembling* portrays Abraham, because of his willingness to sacrifice his son, Isaac, on divine command, not as a great *moral* figure, comparable to Agememnon or Brutus the Younger, who also were willing to sacrifice their offspring, but as a divinely inspired *religious* figure. It would not be difficult to show that Kierkegaard's reading is quite arbitrary and that in the end Abraham's action in sacrificing an animal instead of a human being testifies to the supremacy of morality, to the birth of a new moral insight or judgment for which he and we as individual human beings must take responsibility, and not to a pious, unreasoning acceptance of a command from an allegedly divine power.

But the argument is unnecessary. For it should be clear that if like Solzhenitsyn we wish to unite mankind in the defense of rational freedom, in the preservation of a free society, it is not necessary to agree on first and last things about God, immortality, or any other transcendental dogma. Actually the great majority of mankind do not subscribe to the Judeo-Christian faith—they are Hindus, Buddhists, Confucians, Shintoists, naturalists, and animists. Religion is a private matter, and religious freedom means the right to believe or disbelieve in one, many, or no gods. If we wish to unify or even universalize the struggle for freedom, I propose that we find a set of ethical principles on which human beings can agree regardless of their differing presuppositions, a set of common human needs and human rights that will permit human beings of different cultures, if not to live and *help* each other to live, at least to live and *let* each other live. What unites Solzhenitsyn and Sakharov and us with them—our love of human freedom and our desire to preserve a free society—is more important than any of our differences. Solzhenitsyn's strategy divides us in the common struggle by his criticism of secular rational humanism.

A Great Moral Prophet

Despite my differences with Solzhenitsyn on the matters I have mentioned and on others also, I regard him as one of the great moral prophets of our time. After all, what is it that has moved him to his thunderous evocations of despair with the values and absence of values in the West? It is his observation, repeated in various ways, that the relatively free areas of the world are becoming progressively weaker *vis-à-vis* the totalitarian powers and their assorted varieties of Gulag Archipelagos. And he has been struck to the very heart of his being by the growing feeling among some leading intellectual figures of the West, like George Kennan, that "we cannot apply moral criteria to politics," and that since resistance may lead to a universal conflict in which the survivors will envy the dead, the West starting with the United States must "begin unilateral disarmament."

And what if the enemies of a free society are not inspired by this spirit of Christian submission? What if, interpreting pacifism and appeasement in good Leninist fashion as an expression of cultural decadence, they move to take over the remaining centers of freedom? Better that, says George Kennan, than the consequences of resistance. Echoing Bertrand Russell in his last years, Kennan proclaimed, in his famous interview in the *New York Times,* "Rather Red, than Dead." Solzhenitsyn finds that this is a mood not far below the surface in Western Europe and other areas. In moments of crisis we find it expressed in many ways. How often have I heard variations on the themes "It is better to live on your knees than die on your feet" and "It is better to be a live jackal than a dead lion."

Now, for one thing—although Solzhenitsyn does not say this—Kennan's and Russell's strategy of ultimate surrender may not work in a world where two super-Communist powers possess nuclear weapons with which they threaten each other. We may first become Red and still end up dead!*

---

*It is noteworthy that Bertrand Russell, when he had reached the age of Socrates, still gave precedence to freedom over mere survival—even after the hydrogen bomb had been invented. "Terrible as a new world war would be, I still for my part should prefer it to a universal Communist empire" (*New York Sunday Times Magazine,* September 27, 1953). Subsequently he was to defame those who defended this position.

As I read him, Solzhenitsyn is saying something different. He claims that our greatest danger is the loss of moral nerve, the loss of will power, the loss of belief that some things are morally more important than mere life itself, and that without such belief, weapons, "no matter how great the accumulation, cannot help the West overcome its loss of will" to defend free institutions. In one of the memorable sentences in his Harvard address, he quietly says, "To defend oneself, one must also be ready to die"—and the context shows that by this he means the defense of our free institutions as our ultimate concern. There is a profound historical and psychological truth here. The lean and hungry hordes ready to die have always triumphed over those who have sought primarily to save their goods or to save their necks. (Not infrequently they lost both, and their honor as well.) Deny Solzhenitsyn's proposition and what conclusion must one draw? That survival is the be-all and end-all of life, the ultimate value. But if we are prepared to sacrifice all our basic values for mere survival, there is no infamy we will not commit. The result would be a life morally unworthy of man's survival.

Solzhenitsyn's abiding message is that if we renew our moral courage, our dedication to freedom, we can avoid both war and capitulation in the grim days ahead. Our choice is not between being "Red or dead"—provided we are prepared to stake our lives, if necessary, on freedom. For we are dealing not with totalitarian madmen but with Leninists who worship at the altar of history, who believe their triumph is inevitable without war, and who, by virtue of every principle of their ideology, will never initiate a world war unless they are certain they will win it. Our task is to be strong enough to prevent their belief in such a certainty. Why should they risk a war when they are gaining power and growing stronger without war, using other nations as mercenaries in local military engagements?

One need not endorse Solzhenitsyn's specific political judgments to agree with him that so long as the West remains strong enough to preclude any guarantee of totalitarian victory, and so long as it recognizes that the essential moral element in that strength is the willingness to risk one's life in the defense of freedom, there will be no world war. World peace, which has existed under the balance of terror, will be preserved as we rely on multilateral disarmament and the hope of evolutionary peaceful changes in totalitarian societies. We have seen Fascist countries become transformed into imperfect democracies without war. So long as we keep our guard up and do not capitulate *à la* Kennan or Russell, *perhaps* someday totalitarian Communist countries may through internal development democratize themselves without war.

Differing as profoundly as I do with Solzhenitsyn about so much, I am nonetheless confident that he would agree with a short answer I have made to the Kennans and Russells of this world in the form of a thumbnail credo:

"It is better to be a live jackal than a dead lion—for jackals, not men. Men who have the moral courage to fight intelligently for freedom and are prepared to die for it have the best prospects of avoiding the fate both of live jackals and of dead lions. Survival is not the be-all and end-all of a life worthy of man. Sometimes the worst thing we can know about a man is that he has survived. Those who say life is worth living at any cost have already written for themselves an epitaph of infamy, for there is no cause and no person they will not betray to stay alive. Man's vocation should be the use of the arts of intelligence in behalf of human freedom."

HAROLD J. BERMAN

The Weightier Matters of the Law

To THE 10,000 STUDENTS and alumni assembled at the 1978 Harvard commencement, Solzhenitsyn seemed like a man from Mars. Here was a great prophet from another world. He was known to us primarily as one who, in his writings, had powerfully and brilliantly exposed the evils of the Stalin terror. These are the works not of a philosopher or a sociologist but of a writer, in the traditional Russian sense of that word—a novelist or poet who is at the same time a seer, one who looks into the soul of a people. Using his great literary talent and prophetic insight to tell the story of the sufferings inflicted upon him and millions of fellow prisoners in the "archipelago" of Soviet labor camps, Solzhenitsyn has also portrayed, in a manner that is characteristically Russian, both the tragic and the heroic side of that cataclysmic experience, its diabolical and at the same time its potentially sanctifying character.

Solzhenitsyn's quality as a writer—his short story entitled "Matryona's House," which is not about the labor camps at all, is one of the great literary gems of our time—is measured by his ability to make us share with him the whole experience of the terror. Having been sentenced as a counter-revolutionary because of some veiled derogatory remarks about Stalin that he wrote in a letter to a friend near the end of World War II, Solzhenitsyn used

---

HAROLD J. BERMAN *is a professor of law at Harvard Law School. His books include "Justice in the U.S.S.R.: An Interpretation of Soviet Law," "The Nature and Functions of Law," and "The Interaction of Law and Religion."*

his mathematical training to devise a mnemonic system for recording in his memory every important detail of life in the camps. To keep even the crudest written report was strictly prohibited; everything had to be committed to memory. The fate of his comrades was impressed like a scar on the tissue of his brain. He swore that he would not let them be forgotten.

His books about the camps are not only, however, a story of those people; they are also a story of the tyranny of the system, especially as that tyranny was manifested in its own inner logic, its internal rationality, indeed, its own perverted legality. We usually think of the camps as being the very opposite of rationality and legality, as the embodiment of arbitrariness. Solzhenitsyn, however, shows us that the arbitrariness of the system was expressed above all in its legalism. Everything was done in the name of the law—some article of the Code, some regulation of the Ministry or of the Chief Administration or of the Director, some rule of the camps that had to be obeyed.

For example, Solzhenitsyn describes the operation of the system of complaints. According to the law, every prisoner was entitled to petition higher authorities if his rights were violated, and all such complaints were to be examined and acted upon. So the prisoner would ask for a pencil and a piece of paper on which to write a complaint. Eventually, he would be given a pencil, but it would hardly write; and a piece of paper, but it was of such a poor quality that it could not be written on, and besides, it was too small. Finally, after tremendous effort, the prisoner wrote out some sort of complaint, which he handed to the investigator or guard—who threw it away, perhaps, or passed it on to someone. Perhaps it eventually disappeared into some file or other. There was never any response. The forms of law were utilized, but in a completely perverse way.

Bureaucratic perversity was connected, in Solzhenitsyn's view, with the emphasis of the system on science and on planning—which was also perverted in practice. The system, by its scientific rationality and by its legalism, "strangles the personality" (as he put it in his Harvard address). The only way to overcome the tyranny of rationality and of legalism was to die to oneself, to give up everything, to give up even the desire for anything for oneself. One of the prisoners says to a camp official: "You can tell old you-know-who-up-there that you only have a power over people so long as you don't take *everything* away from them. But when you have robbed a man of everything, he is no longer in your power, he is free again." So Solzhenitsyn, in James Luther Adams's words, "sees in the brutality and dehumanization of the labor camps the consequences of a rationality that wills one thing and one thing only." Yet he believes that the resources of the human spirit are great enough to overcome even this demonic force.

Having been expelled from his country, Solzhenitsyn continued to publish new volumes of *The Gulag Archipelago* and to work for the victims of Soviet repression. At the same time he spoke out for a new Russia in which the old Russia would be restored, a Christian Russia whose leadership might even be Communist but whose people would be free to maintain their Russian Orthodox faith without political interference, and where a strong sense of spiritual togetherness would be combined with humanitarian aspirations and a sense of national mission.

Although he had been in the United States for several years, the Harvard address was to be Solzhenitsyn's first major expression of his views in this country. We looked forward to it eagerly. Most people, no doubt, anticipated that he would now praise America for those strengths and virtues it offers in opposition to the Soviet system: above all, our freedom and our law. Imagine our dismay when, instead, he attacked the things we cherish most, and charged that those very freedoms which we oppose to the brutality of the Stalin terror, those very laws which are genuine laws and not the perverted laws of the Stalin terror, that very humanism, that tolerance, that pluralism, which we suppose to be the very things needed to save us from brutality and dehumanization—that these strengths and virtues, as we conceive them, are in fact the root cause of our decadence, our materialism, our criminality, our superficiality, our spiritual exhaustion, our "loss of civic courage," our breakdown of leadership. And imagine our further dismay when he urged upon us the very values of sacrifice and self-discipline and collective will, our subordination to authority, and of common faith that we in America have long associated with the Communist system.

Ten thousand people cheered and applauded the speech. When they went home and thought about it, however, many of them changéd their minds. Soon letters began to appear in the press denouncing the speech and calling the speaker a false prophet. The press itself was not at all pleased that the great man had said it was irresponsible and corrupt and dangerous. The legal profession was not pleased to be told that our laws are cold, hard, and impersonal, and that they are a source of conformism and even corruption. Youth—and ex-youth—were shocked at the assertion that it was lack of civil courage that had induced us to withdraw from the Vietnam war. The clergy was pleased, but the professors were not, to hear a call for a return to faith in a Supreme Being.

A *New York Times* editorial charged Solzhenitsyn with having an "obsessive personality" and a "messianic complex." That newspaper's senior columnist, James Reston, quoted Solzhenitsyn's statement: "A fact which cannot be disputed is the weakening of human beings in the West while in the East [owing to their spiritual training in suffering] they are becoming firmer and stronger. . . ." Reston, who is normally quite calm, responded: "This from the author of the unspeakable tortures of the Soviet prisons and psychiatric wards? This is 'a fact which cannot be disputed?' The hell it can't!" Solzhenitsyn seemed to have touched a raw nerve.

How the West Lost Heart

When one studies Solzhenitsyn's Harvard address carefully, it turns out to be much more complex and difficult to understand than is generally realized. The spiritual exhaustion of the West, our lack of courage, our decadence, is only one major theme. And it is not a simple one.

Within this theme there are four main points. The *first* is that modern Western states were founded on a belief in the pursuit of

happiness. Here Solzhenitsyn cited, of course, the American Declaration of Independence; however, he mistakenly identified the
concept of happiness in that document with the possession of
material goods. With regard to the pursuit of happiness (so defined), Solzhenitsyn made two subpoints: that the desire for more
material goods does not in fact bring happiness and, more
important, that this desire is an obstacle to free spiritual
development—more particularly, it is an obstacle to the willingness to risk one's "precious life" in the defense of common
values. In a society raised in the cult of material well-being, Solzhenitsyn said, there is little readiness to die to defend one's
country.

It may seem like carping to point out that Solzhenitsyn confused eighteenth-century and twentieth-century concepts of happiness, and that what the pursuit of happiness meant to the framers of the Declaration of Independence was really a secular form
of blessedness or salvation, namely, an aspiration to the good life.
It is by no means unimportant to recognize, however, that the
pursuit of material welfare has come to mean something quite
different in the twentieth century from what it previously meant.
In nineteenth-century America it meant working against heavy
odds for a decent standard of living, one that would release time
and energy for education and for the improvement of social conditions. Solzhenitsyn neglected to say that the search for material
goods may have a spiritual value under conditions of hardship that
is entirely lacking under conditions of abundance. Moreover, the
notion that there is a necessary conflict between the pursuit of
happiness and the willingness to risk one's life for defense is
disproved by the example of the framers of the Declaration of
Independence, who for the sake of life, liberty, and the pursuit of
happiness were willing to pledge their lives, their fortunes, and
their sacred honor.

Solzhenitsyn's *second* main point is that our pursuit of material
goods is linked with legalism. In Western society, he stated, "the
limits of human rights and justice are determined by a system of
laws." A legal solution is considered to be "the supreme
solution"—"if a man is proven right by law, nothing more is

required." So the selfishness of Western man is closely connected, in Solzhenitsyn's view, with his reverence for law. I shall return later to the concepts of law and legalism implicit in this view.

The *third* main point is that both the selfishness and the legalism of the West are linked to a larger philosophical concept that Solzhenitsyn called "rationalistic humanism," or "anthropocentrism." Rationalistic humanism, he said—that is, the worship of man and his material needs—which was responsible for the rise of the West in the centuries of the Renaissance and of the Enlightenment, is now the cause of its impending downfall.

Here Solzhenitsyn committed a serious factual error about Western history—one that is widely committed in the West itself, though it has been exposed by virtually all professional historians. He contrasted the materialism of modern Western man from the time of the Renaissance with the spirituality of medieval Western man in the preceding period. He stated that in the Middle Ages spirituality predominated over man's physical nature, and a sense of man's inherent sinfulness and weakness predominated over his self-affirmation and sense of power. The waning of the Middle Ages, according to Solzhenitsyn, was due to exhaustion caused by the despotic oppression of man's physical nature.

In fact, however, it is well known that the High Middle Ages, the period from the late eleventh to the fifteenth century, was a time of great self-confidence and of great energy and expansion. It was a time of dynamic growth in the arts and architecture, in literature and scholarship, as well as in agriculture and industry. Thousands of cities were founded. Commerce flourished. The universities were established. The Gothic cathedrals were built. Sophisticated legal systems were created both in the ecclesiastical and in the secular polity.

Moreover, Solzhenitsyn's notion that it was in the modern period of "rationalistic humanism," dating from the Renaissance, that the existence of intrinsic evil in man was denied, runs into the difficulty that this was the same period in which Protestantism, with its emphasis on man's sinfulness, emerged and flourished. And surely the framers of the United States Constitution, though they were men of the Enlightenment, strongly believed in the intrinsic evil of human nature—indeed, it was to restrain man's natural greed and lust for power that a government of laws, a government of checks and balances, was created.

Solzhenitsyn's *fourth* main point is quite different from the first three, and even contradictory to them. Two hundred years ago, when American democracy was created, he stated, "all individual human rights were granted on the grounds that man is God's creature." Freedom was then conditioned on religious responsibility. Even fifty years ago, freedom was understood in the context of "the moral heritage of the Christian centuries, with their great reserves of mercy and sacrifice." Today, however, there is a despiritualized and irreligious humanism, both in the East and in the West. We have lost the belief in a "Supreme Complete Entity" that once restrained our passions and our irresponsibility. We have placed too much hope in political and social reform only to find we were being deprived of our spiritual life—in the East by the Communist party and in the West by commercial interests.

This is the real crisis. Solzhenitsyn had started his speech with the words "Our world is divided." He had gone on to say that it was divided among a variety of civilizations—the West, China, India, the Muslim world, Africa, Russia. He had then criticized the West for its "spiritual exhaustion." But near the end of his speech, the splits in the world seemed less terrible than the similarity of the disease plaguing most of its parts. At the end, the speech was not essentially about "The Exhausted West," the title given when it was published in *Harvard Magazine;* nor was it essentially about "A World Split Apart," as it was later entitled when published in book form. It was, instead, a prophetic utterance about the spiritual condition of the whole of mankind, East and West, South and North: a mankind threatened with spiritual suffocation, dehumanized and despiritualized.

In this predicament, mankind's greatest need, Solzhenitsyn said, is voluntary, inspired self-restraint; only this will enable it to rise above the tidal wave of materialism that is engulfing it. His emphasis here on self-restraint is comparable to his earlier emphasis, in his 1970 Nobel Prize speech, on the role of art and poetry and beauty in raising the level of man's spiritual consciousness. At that time he spoke of the need for freedom of the creative arts and literature, quoting the great line that Dostoevsky put in the mouth of Prince Myshkin in *The Idiot:* "The world will be saved by beauty." There is no inconsistency between the two speeches in this respect. An attack on the abuses and excesses of freedom is entirely compatible with a belief in freedom. This is a point missed by many critics of Solzhenitsyn's Harvard address. What is meant by freedom is another matter. For Solzhenitsyn, freedom means primarily moral and spiritual freedom; legal freedoms—legal rights—are seen by him as, at best, a means to that end. This, too, is a matter to which I shall return.

The Harvard address concludes with the prophecy that the world "has reached a historic turning point, equal in importance to the turn from the Middle Ages to the Renaissance." We shall have to rise, Solzhenitsyn states, "to a new, higher vision, to a new level of life, where our physical nature will not be condemned as in the Middle Ages—but, even more important, our spiritual nature will not be trampled upon as in modern times." A new anthropological stage has been reached. "No one on earth has any other way left but—upward."

Two Views of Law

We can best sort out the paradoxes in Solzhenitsyn's Harvard address, best explain the self-contradictions, by tracing his concept of law to its sources in Russian Orthodox Christianity and in Russian and Soviet experience, and by contrasting that concept with the concept of law embodied in Western Christianity and in the Western legal tradition.

Rare is the commencement speaker who does not pay tribute to our Constitution and to our legal system, or at least to the Supreme Court. Distinctions may be made between the great constitutional principles and the ways in which they have been applied. The Supreme Court may be criticized for departing from values and policies of an earlier period. A call may be sounded for changes in particular laws. But to attack law itself as a value, as a standard, as a bond of our unity—this is unheard of! Yet this is what Solzhenitsyn seemed to be doing. No wonder there was a strong reaction from our "opinion leaders." Some of them even went so far as to see in the speech a defense of totalitarianism. But that, surely, is a misunderstanding. When Solzhenitsyn attacked the sensationalism and irresponsibility of the press, for example, he was by no means suggesting the desirability of censorship or other legal controls. On the contrary, he has little faith in legal controls of any kind. He was calling, rather, for self-restraint. The differences between Solzhenitsyn and most of his critics are subtler and deeper than most of the critics seem to realize.

Solzhenitsyn accuses the West, and especially the United States, of attaching to law a moral value that it does not deserve. He does not deny—on the contrary, he affirms—the necessity of having a legal order for the protection of society against arbitrariness and oppression. "Having spent all my life under a Communist rule," he states, "I can testify that a society with no objective legal scale is terrible indeed." However, "a society with no other scale but the legal one is less than worthy of man." Law belongs, in his view, to a lower order of moral and social life, and the West has given itself over to that lower order. Therefore the West offers no satisfactory model for "us," that is, for the Russians.

Solzhenitsyn's attack on the morality of law, or on law as the embodiment of moral values, reflects a form of antinomianism—"anti-lawism"—whose roots are deep in Russian history and culture. In traditional Russian Orthodox Christianity, law is sharply contrasted with grace, with faith, and with love. Law is thought to be hard, cold, impersonal, formal, intellectual; it is connected only with guilt and with punishment. Such antinomianism does not distinguish between a mechanical "legalism" that proceeds on the basis of technicalities and a creative, purposive "legality" that proceeds from a sense of justice. Indeed, there is no special word for "legalism" or "legalistic" in Russian; the same words must be used for "legalism" and "legality," for "legalistic" and "legal." When Solzhenitsyn speaks of law, he speaks only of the letter of the law, which kills, never of the spirit of the law, which gives life.

An important part of Russian spiritual and cultural tradition has been its stress on informal, spontaneous relations within the group, on togetherness, or what in Russian Christianity is called *sobornost'*, "conciliarity," community spirit. Prior to the latter part of the nineteenth century, this was associated in Russian history with an abhorrence of formal adjudication and, indeed, of all legal relations. The Russian church has always denounced Western Christianity for its legalism. The nineteenth-century Slavophile Ivan Kireevsky wrote scornfully, "In the West, brothers make contracts with brothers." In Russia, on the contrary, there should be no need for contracts at all, since all men should be brothers. Similarly, Dostoevsky's Grand Inquisitor can justify social institutions only as a "correction" of Jesus' work; they necessarily sacrifice the person to society, the unique to the statistical. They necessarily contradict the original Christian faith. Solzhenitsyn follows in Dostoevsky's path when he talks about the spiritual life of the unique person and disparages general rules that apply to large numbers. "Whenever the tissue of life is woven of legalistic [in Russian *iuridicheskie,* meaning also "legal" or "juridical"] relations," Solzhenitsyn states, "there is an atmosphere of moral mediocrity, paralyzing man's noblest impulses."

Certainly Solzhenitsyn was justified in warning us against the dangers of too great a reliance upon law, and especially against the exaltation of our legal system, our beloved Constitution, as an ultimate value, an end in itself, the highest standard of our collective life. This is, indeed, a form of idolatry—to worship a man-made thing, to glorify it for its own sake. Our reverence for law is justified only if law is seen as pointing to something higher than itself.

Perhaps he was also justified in charging that in the West personal morality is too often based upon legal standards. Here, however, his examples were not very satisfactory. One was the example of an oil company that purchases an invention of a new form of energy in order to suppress its use. Solzhenitsyn cited this to illustrate the statement: "One almost never meets with voluntary self-restraint. Everyone tries to go to the very limits of the legal framework." The second example, given to illustrate the same statement, was that of a food manufacturer who poisons his product to make it last longer; "after all, people are free not to buy it." These two examples show that conduct which is legal may nevertheless be immoral (although the word "poisons" suggests that the food manufacturer's conduct was in fact both immoral and illegal). But they are surely not examples of legalism. On the contrary, they suggest the need for more stringent *legal* controls of private economic activity. In England, for example, the law authorizes the government to make an unused patent available to others who are willing and able to exploit it.

Other examples of alleged legalism were supplied by Solzhenitsyn in a letter to the student organizers of a conference on law and religion. One was an example of a false claim for personal injury: a car was barely touched by another, and the driver falsely claimed severe injury to his back. The other was a case of a person who, being in a situation of danger, was rescued by a passerby and who then sued his rescuer on the false charge of having caused the predicament from which in fact the rescuer had saved him. These examples, too, seem to reflect a serious misunderstanding of the nature of legal rules and the differences between personal morality and social morality. Presumably it is socially desirable to have a system of insurance against losses caused by injuries. However, such a system is subject to abuse by unconscionable people who present inflated claims. A person who makes an inflated claim is, of course, committing both an immoral and an illegal act. If what Solzhenitsyn is saying is that many people in the United States think anything is morally justified "provided you can get away with it," then this is a charge against our standards of morality, not against either our legal system or our faith in our legal system.

No doubt there are other better examples, however, to support Solzhenitsyn's contention that we have identified our moral values too closely with legal standards. We say, for instance, that there is nothing *wrong* if an employer pays his workers the minimum wage, even if it is too low and he can afford to pay them more, since he is acting within the law. And many people would say they are entirely justified morally in not paying a debt after the legal time-period has passed within which a claim must be made. Here we are indeed guilty of confusing legality with morality.

Yet it is doubtful that even such examples as these really demonstrate that Americans today are a people who put too much faith in the law and who identify what is legally right with what is morally right. If anything, they show a certain cynicism about the law. And, in fact, Americans increasingly seem to be a people who do *not* believe in the law, and who are inclined to break the law whenever they can do so with impunity. Judge Lois Forer of the Philadelphia Court of Common Pleas has written that we are a nation of scofflaws—at all levels, rich and poor, old and young, men and women, white and black. If this is so, the message we need to hear is not that we overvalue law but that we undervalue it. We need to recover our sense of the historical rootedness of our law in our moral and religious tradition: this is connected with Solzhenitsyn's fourth point. That recovery would help us reform our legal system in the direction of greater humaneness and greater social justice without making it an object of idolatry.

The Need for Reconciliation of Values

It is likely, however, that Solzhenitsyn was speaking primarily not to us but rather to his own people. At one point he stated that he does not consider the West as it is today "a model for my country." "I could not recommend your society as an ideal for the transformation of ours. . . . True, a society cannot remain in such an abyss of lawlessness as our country is in. But it also is demeaning for it to remain in a state of such soulless, polished legalism as yours is in. The human soul, which for decades suffered under coercion, longs for things higher, warmer, purer than those offered by today's Western mass existence."

This was not the proper time or place for Solzhenitsyn to present in any detail his vision of the future of his people. Yet whatever that vision may be, it is strange that there is apparently no place in it for a loftier concept of legality than he was willing to suggest. Surely what is needed in the Soviet Union is not just an "objective legal scale," or the elimination of the "abyss of lawlessness." In fact, since Stalin's time the Soviet Union—despite its repression of dissent—has moved far toward establishing a legal regime characterized by objectivity and generality. The terror is gone. People are no longer sentenced merely on the ground that they are "enemies of the people," or convicted without a trial, or tried merely on the basis of denunciations. Permissible areas of criticism of leaders' policies have been greatly expanded. The country has been opened to broad contact with foreigners. Solzhenitsyn is quite wrong in implying that there is still no lawfulness, no objective legal scale, in the Soviet Union.

Yet much is still wrong with the Soviet legal system. There is still severe *legal* repression of freedom, and there is still much legally sanctioned injustice. Moreover, there are still perversions of legality, though on a greatly reduced scale. Also, outside the law there is much selfishness, arbitrariness, and corruption. What is needed in the Soviet Union, as everywhere, is not only the kind of religious spirit that Solzhenitsyn calls for—the spirit of generosity and of service and sacrifice, the sense of a higher human destiny—but also the kind of political, economic, and social structure, indeed, the kind of legal institutions, in whose soil such a spirit may take root and flourish.

Here Jesus' famous attack upon "the lawyers" is highly relevant. "Woe to you lawyers," he said, "for you tithe mint and anise and cummin and neglect the weightier matters of the law, which are justice and mercy and good faith. These you ought to do, without neglecting the others." Too often the last sentence of this passage is left out. What the whole passage says is first, that the heart of the law is "justice and mercy and good faith," and second, that the lesser matters, the technicalities, the taxes, the "mint and anise and cummin," are also important, although they should be subordinated to the main purpose.

The relation between law, on the one hand, and justice or love, on the other, is not—need not be—one of antagonism. Law is, in fact, a way of translating both justice and love into social situations involving large numbers of people. The individual person who sees a man lying injured by the wayside should be inspired by love of neighbor to help him; a law regulating the provision of medical care and compensation for persons who suffer injuries is a way of generalizing that neighborly spirit. Of course, when society acts, rather than the individual person, the passionate element, the heroic element, the sacrificial element, is to some extent reduced. But it is by no means eliminated. Too sharp a contrast between the personal and the social does a disservice to both. Law is concerned with both, just as religion is concerned with both.

It is no doubt a good thing for Russians, and not only for Americans, to be told that the American way of life is not an appropriate "model" for their future, just as it is good not only for Americans and others but also for the Soviets to hear that the socialist system as practiced in the U.S.S.R. has lost its appeal even for the downtrodden of most other countries of the world. It is good news that the time for such models has passed, and that each country, each culture, must develop its own images of the future. By the same token, however, the perpetuation of the Russian Slavophile dream of an Eastern Christian kingdom in which *sobornost'* and spirituality reign and Western "legalism" and "contractualism" have no place—is also anachronistic.

The predominant emphasis on spirituality and other-worldliness that Solzhenitsyn attributes to Western Man in the Middle Ages is a phenomenon of Christianity in the first thousand years of its history, both in the East and in the West, when the monastic life was the only escape from a world seen to be in perpetual decay. Eastern Christianity has to a considerable extent preserved that emphasis, at least in comparison with Western Christianity, which since the Gregorian revolution of the late eleventh century has stressed the mission of the Church to reform the world, not only through faith but also through structures and institutions. Thus the West, together with other parts of the world that have come under its influence, has lived out a second thousand years in which legal and other structural or institutional values have often been raised to a position of predominance.

Both East and West have suffered immeasurably from these dualisms—from the split in values between the eternal and the temporal, grace and law, spirit and matter, passion and reason, the spontaneous and the planned, the sacred and the just. Today we know that to attack one set of these values in the name of the other is to threaten the integrity both of the person and of society. What is required is not a rejection of the positive values either of the East or of the West but rather a new integration of them. Indeed, not only East and West, in the traditional meanings of those names, but all the cultures of the world must draw on one another's resources if mankind is to enter the new stage to which Solzhenitsyn calls us.

RICHARD PIPES

In the Russian Intellectual Tradition

THOSE WHO, LIKE MYSELF, had listened to Solzhenitsyn in the Harvard Yard on that drizzly June afternoon carried away the impression that we had heard a devastating attack on the contemporary West—for its loss of courage, its self-indulgence, its self-deception. It was as if the speaker, a refugee from hell, had excoriated us, denizens of purgatory, for not living in paradise.

A subsequent reading of the address, however, suggested that its message lay on a more abstract historico-philosophical plane. Chaotic in structure (it must have been written in fits and starts), the speech does not reach its center of gravity until nearly the end, in a place where the reader expects a summary. Here Solzhenitsyn addresses himself to his central concern, the underlying causes of what he perceives to be the malaise of the entire modern world, West as well as East.

Solzhenitsyn's principal points can be summarized as follows (more schematically than he does it himself, for he leaves much unsaid):

Man is inherently a corrupt being, the "carrier of inner evil" (all quotations from the speech are my own translations). The rise first of humanism and then of the Enlightenment has led Western society to renounce this truth, and to replace it with the false and pernicious idea of man's perfectibility. The consequence has been

RICHARD PIPES *is professor of history at Harvard University and former director of its Russian Research Center. Among his books are "The Formation of the Soviet Union," "Russia Under the Old Regime," and "Europe Since 1815."*

a culture centered on man as a self-sufficient (autonomous) creature dedicated to the "cult of earthly well-being," with all that this
idea implies, including limitless self-indulgence. Through the
medium of socialism, the "humanist autonomous irreligious consciousness" has penetrated Russia, producing Communism. (Although Solzhenitsyn has nothing but scorn for the theory of the
"convergence" of Western and Communist societies, he firmly
believes in their close spiritual affinity and blames Russia's Communism on the West.) The culture of humanism has led to a state
of perpetual discontent in the West, and in the East, to tyranny
and genocide. The cultures of East and West have this in common: they deny man's inner evil. Although its manifestations
happen to be much more repugnant in the East, there is really not
much to choose from when one confronts these two systems,
locked in mortal combat. The probability is that the Eastern var-
iant will triumph, because its leaders are more determined and
less scrupulous. The West is doomed. In the long run, however, if
mankind survives the coming catastrophe (probably a non-nuclear
war), a higher civilization will emerge that will satisfy, in just
measure, both the spiritual and the physical needs of man: a synthesis of the Middle Ages and modernity, as it were.

The general line of this argument is familiar to anyone who is
acquainted with the history of Russian thought and literature.
Indeed, as we shall note, in places Solzhenitsyn uses virtually the
same language as his nineteenth-century forerunners. This fact
emphasizes the remarkable continuity of Russian intellectual history, especially its conservative strain, to which Solzhenitsyn in-
dubitably belongs. Each generation of Russians seems to discover
afresh the same answers, partly because of the hold on their imagination of Orthodox Christianity, and partly because the problems
that they confront decade after decade remain strikingly similar.

The central postulate of Solzhenitsyn's case—the corrupt nature of man and, its corollary, the futility of manipulating his
social and political environment—is axiomatic for all Russian
conservatives. Two hundred years ago, in the reign of Catherine
II, this was the issue that caused the conservative Novikov and
Russia's first radical, Radishchev, to go their separate ways. In

the reign of Alexander I, Karamzin raised his powerful voice against the reforms of Speranskii in the name of this doctrine: "What matters are not forms, but men." Later, in the middle of the nineteenth century, to the claim of Turgenev's "nihilist" Bazarov (in *Fathers and Sons*) that "in a well-constructed society it will be quite irrelevant whether man is stupid or wise, evil or good," the conservative Dostoevsky responded: "The main thing is to love others as oneself—that is the main thing, and this is all, and nothing more is needed. As soon as you know this, everything will be arranged." On the eve of World War I, the symposium *Vekhi* ("landmarks") shook Russian opinion with the thesis that the intellectual and moral improvement of man had to precede political and social reform. One's attitude toward this question—whether or not human improvement takes precedence over social reform—determines one's place in the Russian intellectual tradition.

As many observers have already noted, Solzhenitsyn's conservatism is Slavophile in character. There are, indeed, many similarities between his criticism of the West, with its prognosis of the West's inevitable decline, and the historical philosophy of the Slavophiles. But the differences are no less striking. In its original form, as popularized in the 1840s and 1850s, Slavophilism contained strong liberal elements. Suffice it to say that its adherents admired England and supported the Great Reforms of Alexander II, including the reform of the judiciary, based on Western models; they also advocated untrammeled freedom of speech, which so annoys Solzhenitsyn. These men were addicted to a *Schwärmerei* peculiar to Romanticism, collecting folk songs and dressing up in seventeenth-century costumes.

Solzhenitsyn's Slavophilism is of a different vintage. It is of a later variety that first arose in the 1870s in response to the emergence in Russia of revolutionary radicalism: its pathos is antidemonic. The outstanding spokesmen of this kind of conservative nationalism were Dostoevsky and his friend Constantine Pobedonostsev, the *éminence grise* of late Imperial Russia. They, it seems to me, are Solzhenitsyn's direct intellectual ancestors. To convince oneself of this affinity, one has only to take in hand

Pobedonostsev's *Reflections of a Russian Statesman* (1896): both in tone and in argument, Solzhenitsyn's Harvard speech is so close to this work that with only minor changes whole passages could be seamlessly incorporated into Pobedonostsev's book.

It is the central theme of Dostoevsky's great novels that the hubris of humanistic rationalism—what Solzhenitsyn calls the "autonomy of man from any superior power"—inexorably leads to crime. Morality from which religion has been extracted causes Raskolnikov to kill an old woman money-lender, the young Verkhovenskii to sow the seeds of murder around him, and Ivan Karamazov to inspire the assassination of his own father. For Dostoevsky, socialism and communism were natural and inevitable offshoots of liberalism, just as they are for Solzhenitsyn. It is pure Dostoevsky when Solzhenitsyn tells us that "humanism, which has entirely lost its Christian heritage," cannot withstand the challenge of radicalism and ends up in communism—a system which for him signifies murder on a mass scale.

The affinity between Solzhenitsyn and his forerunners from the archconservative reign of Alexander III becomes apparent when we compare his statements on Western law and journalism with corresponding passages from Pobedonostsev's *Reflections*.

Time and again, Solzhenitsyn returns to attacks on Western legality as an empty, inhuman formalism that is capable of allowing the criminal to go free and preventing the victim from obtaining redress, all the time enriching the lawyer. "[Western] laws are so complicated," Solzhenitsyn complains, "that an ordinary man is helpless dealing with them without a specialist." Pobedonostsev (who, incidentally, was an eminent jurist) would have concurred: "The simple man cannot know the law, or vindicate his rights. . . . He falls into the hands of attorneys, the sworn mechanics of the machine of justice." Like Solzhenitsyn, Pobedonostsev assailed the Western legal system for concentrating on the "technical" aspects of the law at the expense of "justice."

There are in Solzhenitsyn's speech also virulent attacks on the Western press for its arrogance, superficiality, and censorship of unfashionable thoughts. He then demands: "What is the responsibility of the journalist and newspaper before the reading public or history?. . .Under what electoral law has [the Western press] been elected. . .?" And here is Pobedonostsev: "Who are these representatives of this terrible power, Public Opinion? Whence derives their right and authority to rule in the name of the community. . .?" He answers: "The journalist. . .derives his authority from no election."

Such examples could be multiplied. The two writers, nearly a century apart, show the same contempt for Western parliamentary institutions ("The Great Falsehood of Our Time" for Pobedonostsev, the subject of a derisive aside for Solzhenitsyn) and for the whole institutional apparatus protecting the political and civil freedoms of Western man. Not the least quality they have in common is the fundamental vice of Russian conservative (and radical) intellectuals, that of never conceding a point to an adversary—a vice that is second in its debilitating effect on Russian life only to the habit of spinning thoughts about social and political matters without any consideration of their practicability or acceptability to the mass of mankind.

Like everything he writes, Solzhenitsyn's Harvard address shines with incorruptible courage. Surely it took courage to admonish a Harvard audience, of all audiences, for the participation of American "activists" in the "betrayal" of Vietnam and Cambodia. And how much else he says that needs saying and is usually not said because of the tyranny of conformism! His contemptuous reference to the "short-sighted politician who had hurriedly signed the Vietnam capitulation"; his scorn for the political amoralism of America's "very prominent figures" who, by confusing good and evil, truth and lie, promote the triumph of "Absolute Evil"; his description of government functionaries who seek to justify their cowardice with intellectual and even moral arguments—all this was well said and was perceived as such by the Harvard audience, which, for all its bewilderment, responded from time to time to its tormentor's exhortations with bursts of self-conscious applause.

And yet, like many conservatives, Solzhenitsyn is far better at diagnosing ills than at providing remedies. In the end, his kind of conservatism, like that of his *ancien régime* predecessors, strikes me as unconvincing, and this for two reasons.

His criticism of the spiritual corruption and cowardice of Western society, correct as it is, tells only half the story. It is incontestably true that the American press is nowhere as open a forum of opinion as it pretends to be, and that it has arrogated itself a great deal of arbitrary power. But still it was this very same press that rescued Solzhenitsyn from the Soviet police, made it possible for him to find refuge in America, and broadcast his Harvard address to all ends of the globe. Admittedly, our legal formalism can be exasperating and provides too good a living for too many lawyers: nevertheless, it merits saying that our soulless "formal" legalism has prevented in America the establishment of a Gulag system—something that the Slavophile idea of "humane" justice as above the "cold" law has dismally failed to do in Russia. For all the material self-indulgence evident in our society, indeed often repelling and destructive of spiritual life, I believe Americans are more charitable and more given to good works than are ordinary Russians, whose poverty and insecurity forces them to fend for themselves, allowing neither time nor mind to help others. Every dark phenomenon of Western culture has also its bright side—the product, ultimately, of those very qualities of our life that Solzhenitsyn so criticizes, namely freedom, legality, and well-being.

But Solzhenitsyn seems wrong on a still deeper level, where at stake is the highest good as he perceives it, the ultimate goal of our life on earth: "moral elevation," or "leaving life a being of a higher order than one had entered it." This end is certainly attainable only by dint of an individual effort and only in an environment where the individual is free—free not only to choose the "right" path but also to err and, through error, to learn. Furthermore, morality is a goal that the individual can realize only in society, and so he requires protection by a system of objective law (not subjective "justice") to save him from perpetual, unregulated conflict with his fellow men. And, finally, "moral elevation" presupposes a certain minimum standard of life, for apart from a handful of saintly natures, human beings cannot dedicate themselves to moral improvement if they are unable to satisfy their basic wants. So, in the end, freedom, law, and well-being are not to be scorned. They are insufficient but still indispensable conditions for that "moral elevation" of man which Solzhenitsyn rightly regards as life's most sublime task.

To attain this end we must accept, even as we try to change, freedom that degenerates into license, legality that constricts, and well-being that turns into an obsessive accumulation and consumption of material goods. Society is not an association for the joint pursuit of virtue, since one man's virtue is another man's iniquity; such a conception inevitably leads to despotism. Rather, society is an environment for the mutual tolerance and restraint of human weaknesses. How paradoxical it is that Western culture, which is alleged to rest on the notion of human perfectibility, makes the broadest provisions for sin, whereas the kind of ideology that Solzhenitsyn espouses, one that deems man incorrigibly evil, insists on his never straying!

WILLIAM H. McNEILL

The Decline of the West

ALEKSANDR SOLZHENITSYN SPEAKS to us as a latter-day representative of the Russian Orthodox tradition. A century ago, Dostoyevsky delivered almost the same message, finding the West profoundly unsatisfactory because of its materialism and legalism. And just as Dostoyevsky's parable of the Grand Inquisitor in *The Brothers Karamazov* offers a compelling caricature of Roman Catholicism, so Solzhenitsyn's Harvard speech gives us an Orthodox Christian's caricature of our society.

Coming as I do from a different tradition, I find some things to agree with (at least in part); but overall I feel that Solzhenitsyn is doing to us what he justly accuses us of doing to others: imposing the values of one style of civilization upon another. One can saddle a cow or a camel, no doubt, but the ride will not resemble a ride on a galloping horse. And just as our values and expectations, applied to Russia or to other culturally autonomous societies, do not shed much light on human motives and behavior there, so, too, an Orthodox expectation and standard of values, applied to the United States or to the West European world at large, does not allow Solzhenitsyn to understand well what goes on among us.

Predictions of the decline of the West are at least two hundred years old. And as Mark Twain said about reports of his death, they have so far proved to be greatly exaggerated. The German philosopher Johann Gottfried von Herder (1744–1803) was

WILLIAM H. MCNEILL *is professor of history at the University of Chicago, where he has taught for more than three decades. His books include "Rise of the West: A History of the Human Community" and "The Shape of European History."*

perhaps the best-known early propagator of this idea. It acquired new vivacity after 1812, when Russian soldiers defeated Napoleon. The fact that Russian soldiers did the same to Hitler in 1943–45 makes comparison of the international politics of our time with the patterns of the early nineteenth century exceptionally interesting.

Yet the fact that West Europeans survived a threat from the Russian east in the nineteenth century is no guarantee that their heirs in the twentieth or the twenty-first century will do the same. Solzhenitsyn's dark sayings should not be dismissed as groundless, though they need not be accepted as more than they are: a powerful caricature of reality, emphasizing aspects of our public life he finds distasteful, without, however, seriously exploring alternatives or their cost.

On the level of action, I find what he says ill thought through. On the one hand, he deplores a decline in our civic courage, and seems to think that we should have demonstrated that courage by fighting on and on in Vietnam until Communism had been defeated—if need be, I suppose, by killing the great majority of the Vietnamese, who clearly ended up by espousing their local brand of national Communism. It seems to me, on the contrary, that we exhibited our civic courage in withdrawing, however belatedly. If American ideology means anything, it requires us to permit majorities in other lands to choose whatever form of government they prefer. If that chosen form turns out to be tyrannous and wicked, if it tramples on human rights, still we must continue to believe that to champion freedom and humanity does not require an armed crusade to enforce an American standard of justice and political propriety.

Solzhenitsyn criticizes us for assuming that all the world is ready and eager to follow in our footsteps, and with this I quite agree. How then can he also wish us to assert our civic courage by enforcing freedom, American-style, in Vietnam, or in other culturally alien parts of the earth? Perhaps the explanation is that his personal experience with the tyranny of Soviet administration makes him eager to see it defeated—everywhere. He does not reflect on the dilemma such a program imposes on a country like the United States: to act as Solzhenitsyn and some American cold warriors once wished us to do would require that the United States take on the militarized, bureaucratically managed, and ideologically oppressive character that he finds so unacceptable in the Soviet Union.

No: on a practical level I see in Solzhenitsyn's speech only incoherence and confusion. Like some lapsed Catholics who as fanatical anti-clericals reproduce in reverse the dogmatism of the faith they reject, Solzhenitsyn carries with him the impress of the Communism he repudiates (as well as of the Orthodoxy he embraces) and seeks to impose on the untidy West the straitjacket of one Truth and one Duty to defend that truth. Russian Communists and Russian Orthodox Christians share this kind of logic. It is, indeed, one of the many things Russian Communism took over from Orthodoxy. Solzhenitsyn therefore, because he remains true to his Russian past, cannot feel comfortable with our messier way of thinking and acting.

Yet, having dismissed his criticisms of our society as a product of misunderstanding and myopia arising from his culture-boundedness, I run the risk of becoming as blind as he. Parading my own culture-boundedness in rebuttal to his and reaffirming the value of pluralism, freedom, law, and the marketplace is a cheap way of dodging the more fundamental issues his speech raises. We are what we are, and not all of it is good or admirable. The sovereignty of the marketplace often results in tawdry goods and even more tawdry amusements. But how can we enforce a different standard of taste on TV programming or a more responsible judgment upon news reports without entrusting unacceptable authority to some kind of censor? And who is to censor the censor? If the common denominator of taste boils down to sex and violence, sex and violence is what we will get as long as the imperatives of the marketplace predominate.

Reducing humanity to its animal level obviously dwarfs human potentiality, and the Christian tradition of repressing rather than flaunting the animal side of human existence appeals to me almost as much as it does to Solzhenitsyn. The emphasis on human animality common in American popular culture during recent decades has simply meant that preoccupations that probably always dominated the consciousness of the great majority of human beings have burst out into the open. Old inhibitions have been scrapped in the interests of gaining a wide audience for whatever the broadcaster seeks to sell. The intellectual and cultural elites that once controlled almost all public forms of communication have been thrust to the margins, without entirely losing their access to the communication media or, perhaps, surrendering very much of their erstwhile audience.

I do not know for sure whether this is true. Perhaps heroic and saintly actions were more likely when they enjoyed a near monopoly of public expression. Easy access to pornography and simulated violence may affect people who would have eschewed such things when they were only whispered about furtively. On the other hand, maybe it makes little statistical difference. The plain fact is that we do not know what the personal and sociological consequences will be of exposure to the kind of programs and news our mass media carry.

I agree with Solzhenitsyn in thinking that the marketplace is an inadequate guide in such things. My problem is that I do not see how to impose my own or anyone else's standard of taste upon the rest of society without becoming as tyrannous as the Soviet authorities are—and perhaps as ineffectual, if animality is as deeply rooted among us as my experience of the U.S. Army seemed to indicate almost forty years ago, at a time when the mass media had only begun to nibble at the edges of the Christian moral heritage.

Far more central to Solzhenitsyn's challenge to us is a proposition he never quite voices, one that apparently lies behind most of his remarks. He seems to be convinced that collective power and secure survival in the world require a unifying ideal or myth in whose defense millions and hundreds of millions of diverse human beings can rally and act as one, led by a statesman who wants, in Solzhenitsyn's words, "to achieve something constructive for his country." Unifying ideals are certainly important. Political action requires them. And the myth that Solzhenitsyn calls "rationalistic humanism" may have lost some of its power to mobilize public action among us, though not nearly so much as Solzhenitsyn (who fervently rejects rationalistic humanism) would have us believe.

For example, the way in which material expectations outrun experience, assuring for most people a continual discontent with whatever level of material affluence they have, proves for Solzhenitsyn the falsity of the ideal. It can just as well be viewed as an example of the invisible hand Adam Smith so much admired, keeping the economic system on its track, no matter what level of wealth and material superfluities a particular society may attain. Material enrichment is, in fact, a very powerful motor to human action. When the possibility is clearly envisioned, men and women of the most diverse societies, with widely discrepant cultural heritages, usually do opt for a line of action that they believe will increase their wealth. The way Western societies have succeeded in achieving levels of wealth superior to those of other peoples is one of the bastions of Western strength in world affairs, though that wealth arouses envy and disdain as well as admiration.

The critical deficiency of our secularized vision of the "true end of man," as inherited from the eighteenth century, seems to me to rest in its individualism. Human beings are social creatures, and happiness depends mainly on effective participation in groups, where shared values and goals, cooperative behavior, and mutual aid can flourish. The critical question, for which we have no sure answer, is: Which group or groups should we belong to? Unfortunately for us, it is also true that the best way to consolidate a group is to pit it against a rival. Heroism and other social behavior flourishes when face to face with an enemy; yet a world split apart, as ours is, risks total destruction in our atomic age.

Earlier, in the nineteenth century and the first half of the twentieth, the Western world resolved these dilemmas by emphasizing national identity above all others. Nationalism went far to countervail the individualism of Western secularist thinking. By identifying with one's nation, one can transcend private deficiencies and disappointments—or so millions came to feel. This sustained national governments and statesmen in their pursuit of power and empire. It gave meaning to life for uprooted urban masses among whom older religious values had faded.

In the second half of the twentieth century, however, the credibility of the national identity is eroding among many Westerners (on both sides of the Atlantic), just as the earlier belief in our human identity as candidates for the Kingdom of Heaven eroded. The resulting vacuum of belief and social support is perhaps what Solzhenitsyn senses when he speaks about our flagging civic courage. To be sure, larger identities, such as "good Europeans" or citizens of Spaceship Earth, have been clearly articulated among us. But such ideals have little hold on the public imagination. Instead, the main thrust of our public life in recent decades has been to divide and subdivide: blacks, Latinos, WASPS, "ethnics," and the like. And for many individuals in our society, quasi-private identities have come forward, such as membership in communes or sects, or an identification with an established institution such as a business corporation, or some other kind of work association.

The older faith in the nation, one and indivisible, and in the values for which it stands has by no means disappeared, any more than Christian and other established religious beliefs have been completely discarded. But the older ideals and identities have certainly lost their self-evident authority. No one can be sure ahead of time how the public will react to some sudden future crisis in which national values and independence might conceivably come into question.

Solzhenitsyn points us toward this question. We in the United States do not know how long the self-evident truths of the Declaration of Independence, as most imperfectly exemplified by the behavior of government officials in their myriad contacts with us, will continue to command sufficiently warm assent that our elected magistrates can mobilize the kind of support needed to compete successfully with other states and political ideologies. Great states and powerful bureaucracies have, in times past, often proved to have feet of clay. This was what happened to the tsarist empire of the nineteenth century, whose armed superiority to other European states in 1815 degenerated into comparative weakness by mid-century, both because the ideals of the tsarist autocracy ceased to command the unambiguous assent of the educated classes in Russia and because of a growing technological obsolescence. The American republic may be moving along a similar path as the twentieth century nears its close.

But before surrendering to despair, or setting out with Solzhenitsyn in search of some new spiritual blaze with which to set the world on fire and transform the basis of political action, I would inquire whether the Soviet Union and other rivals to our own country do not suffer from similar or even more acute internal distresses. Everything I know and believe about the Soviet Union suggests that disenchantment with the ideal of Communism is far more widespread and acute there than is our disenchantment with American political myths. Repressive regimes in other lands presumably provoke similar dissent that, though hidden from public display, affects human behavior just as much.

If the righteousness of the cause is clear, I for one believe that Americans and other citizens of the West will rally again, as their precedessors have done ever since 480 B.C., when a handful of Greek cities turned back a Persian army not because of superior organization or armament but because the Greeks fought willingly, as free men, and in defense of their homelands. A free rallying to the defense of old symbols, tarnished though they may have become, is, I believe, much more likely to happen in a society where many competing voices have checked tyrannous conduct on the part of any one segment of society than it is in a country where a privileged bureaucracy enjoys almost untrammeled authority to order people about.

I agree that the superior power free men can attain is a faith rather than a fact. It has sometimes proved illusory. Citizens have not always rallied in time, and the cause has not always seemed unambiguous enough to justify personal sacrifice and risk-taking. But rather than follow Solzhenitsyn along new and unspecified pathways towards salvation—whether upwards, as he suggests, or downwards or sideways—I prefer to believe that in time of need sufficient unanimity can be achieved within the pluralistic framework of Western society to keep us strong enough to survive.

MICHAEL NOVAK

On God and Man

THE TEXT OF Aleksandr Solzhenitsyn's address at Harvard is, in my view, the most important religious document of our time, more shattering than *Pacem in Terris,* more sharply analytical of the human condition in our century than any word from the World Council of Churches. Out of the long grayness of his own despair, out of the years in which surrender must have seemed attractive and hopelessness realistic, Solzhenitsyn was saved by faith in the power of simple truth. His was not solely a salvation for his soul through faith in Jesus Christ; it was also a ray of light for the entire race of men. He kept his eye upon the need to tell the truth, come what may.

The spiritual center of Solzhenitsyn's analysis of Western society occurs in section five of the speech and again in section fourteen. He says that "the decline of courage is perhaps the most striking feature of the Western world today. . . . This loss of courage is more evident among the ruling and intellectual elites, thus creating an impression that the entire society suffers this decline of courage. . . . Need I remind you that from ancient times a decline in courage has been considered the first symptom of the end?" He then examines the ways in which this loss of courage has occurred. In section fourteen, he returns to the fundamental theme of the inner loss of will: "To defend oneself, one must also be ready to die; but there is little such readiness in a society raised in the cult of affluence. There is then nothing left

---

MICHAEL NOVAK *is resident scholar in religion and public policy at the American Enterprise Institute, Washington, D.C. Among his books are "The Rise of the Unmeltable Ethnics," "Politics: Realism and Imagination," and "Choosing Our King."*

but concessions, procrastinations, and betrayals." And again: "Western thinking has become conservative: the world situation must stay as it is at any cost. There must be no changes. . . . *How is it possible to lose the will to defend yourself to such an extent?"* (italics added). The remainder of Solzhenitsyn's analysis constitutes a profound investigation into the soul and intellectual roots of the West, in search of an answer to that painful question.

Thus Solzhenitsyn observes the malady: loss of courage, lack of will even to defend oneself. He offers two diagnoses of the malady's origin, one centering on the institutions of Western society (notably the law and the press), the other on the vision of man fashioned at the very beginning of the modern era. The mistake "must be at the root," he argues, "at the very foundation of thought in modern times. I refer to the prevailing Western view of the world which was born during the Renaissance and which since the Age of Enlightenment has cast the political mold."

It is at this point that Solzhenitsyn most alarms Western humanists, particularly those who do not believe in God and hold no allegiance to Jewish or Christian thought. Solzhenitsyn seems to be blaming them for the impending catastrophe. If we are to hear him at all, we must deal seriously with this accusation.

The first thing to be said is that Solzhenitsyn's analysis seems classically Catholic. Its general line is that a "wrong turn" was taken in Western history. Even some of Solzhenitsyn's terms (such as "anthropocentrism") resemble those used by the Catholic philosopher Jacques Maritain in *Integral Humanism,* and join a tradition that encompasses many other Christian and Jewish humanists (Paul Tillich, Reinhold Niebuhr, Will Herberg, T. S. Eliot, Christopher Dawson, Emil Fackenheim).

One objection to this interpretation may be that, apart from the "rationalistic humanism" or "humanistic autonomy" that Solzhenitsyn rejects, neither Western liberties nor the creative spirit of productivity and technological invention would have emerged in history. The various theocracies, whether medieval Catholic or later Protestant, or even the theocracies of Russian Orthodoxy better known to Solzhenitsyn, did not always assist the birth of liberty and creativity; on the contrary, they often represented obscurantism, repression, and even the power to halt the course of liberty. In brief, the response to Solzhenitsyn is: We poor secular humanists, with all our faults, have precious little to learn from theocrats or those who (history has taught us) have often enough been forces of reaction. Why should we surrender what we have, problematic as it is, for what appears to be worse?

When Solzhenitsyn speaks of "the disaster of humanistic, autonomous, irreligious consciousness," the unbeliever might, in good conscience, ask for evidence that religious consciousness is not an even more profound calamity. Solzhenitsyn asserts that irreligion "has made man the measure of all things on earth—imperfect man, who is never free of pride, greed, envy, vanity, and dozens of other sins." The unbeliever replies that, on the basis of the evidence, religion seems to do no better. Solzhenitsyn asserts: "We are now being avenged for the mistakes that were not properly appraised at the beginning of the journey. On the way from the Renaissance to our time we have enriched our experience, but we have lost the concept of a Supreme Complete Entity, which once placed a limit on our passions and our irresponsibility. We have placed too much hope in political and social transformations, only to find out that we were being deprived of our most precious possession: our inner life. A party mob attacks it in the East, and the commercial marketplace does the same in the West." Again, the unbeliever replies that a man without God may be just as moral as a believer and have just as profound a spiritual life, perhaps even more profound.

It will seem, then, that Solzhenitsyn is merely being chauvinistic, attempting to impose upon those who think religion is evil the entire blame for the cataclysm that is about to descend upon all, and trying rhetorically to coerce them into accepting his own religious commitments—that is, practicing a kind of spiritual imperialism. Besides, they may think, let him experience some of the more muddleheaded religious spokesmen of the West and then see whether he remains so confident of the power of religion.

Yet all this is, in a way, to miss the point. I do not believe that any honest thinker in the twentieth century can fail to see that there are singularly heroic individuals who, though atheistic or agnostic, have been worthy guides of the human spirit in the midst of despair: men of courage who against Fascism, Stalinism, or whatever other massive evil exhibited no lack of courage, suffered no loss of will. Solzhenitsyn is not, I think, impugning the heroism of spirit possible to the individual atheist or agnostic. He cannot be doing so from a religious point of view, in any case, for as he well recognizes, faith is a gift; without it, before it, a man must do his utmost alone.

Solzhenitsyn is, by contrast, performing a *social* analysis, examining the spiritual life of that large middle band of human life, in which in any society the vast majority, even of its intellectual elite, must live. Solzhenitsyn is observing the malady, not in rare individuals, whom he specifically exempts, but in the typical citizen under typical institutional and symbolic influences. Here, I believe, he makes a stunning observation. There is one major difference—for the more or less middling persons, neither the most heroic nor the most vicious—between a society that is anthropocentric and a society that is theocentric. That difference is that in a society whose moral roots lie solely in individual conscience, a certain diffidence inexorably results: You have your moral convictions, I have mine, who can tell who is right? Directly there follows, barring a great social transformation, a loss of will, of moral certainty, of direction. The Soviets have their system, we have ours, everything depends on your point of view, and so on—it is all, culturally speaking, devastatingly familiar.

At such a point as this, one's judgment of Solzhenitsyn becomes immediately personal. For myself, I think I have previously made clear (in *Belief and Unbelief,* 1965, and *The Experience of Nothingness,* 1970) my respect for the option of unbelief and my esteem for the secular saint. Yet as I grow older I do see the point of such ultimate warnings as those of Dostoyevsky: "If there is no God, everything is permitted," and G. K. Chesterton: "When a man ceases to believe in God, he does not believe in nothing, he believes anything." While brave and strong individuals continue to adhere to honesty, courage, liberty, and compassion, and even to give their lives for values they make central to their being, a *society* based systematically upon the non-existence of God and upon man as the sole measure must, of human necessity, slide further and further into defenselessness and loss of will. For individuals vary. And if some say, "You may prefer *x*, but as for me, I prefer *y*," tolerance demands that they be permitted so to believe. In the vast middle of society, what one generation learns as tolerance, another defines as indifference. Individuals are left to their own moral devices.

John Garvey, commenting upon Solzhenitsyn's Harvard address in *Commonweal* (September 1, 1978), cites the surprise of a college girl when, as a visiting professor, he tried to show how one value can be defended as superior to another. She refused to believe that he actually thought some values were better than others. One of the two professors who regularly taught the class agreed with her, even to the extent of refusing to say that Hitler's values were inferior to those of his opponents. In their minds, Garvey was exhibiting intolerance, arrogance, and cultural chauvinism.

In the vast middle ranges of our society, there are millions who have declared themselves incompetent to make value judgments. They insist that they can choose values only for themselves, and that it would be wrong (immoral? arrogant? coercive?) to "impose" values on, or even to apply one's own values to, others. But this is to refuse to ascend to the moral level, which if it is anything is universal and binding upon all. It is to remain on the level of personal feeling and personal preference. It is to legitimate those who *prefer* torture, rapine, systematic murder, authoritarianism, slavery. Of course, not facing such issues in their daily lives, protected by the defenses around this island of liberty, such defenders of non-discrimination do not see the implications of their own moral vagueness. They believe in "freedom," in "non-coercion," in "keeping institutions off my back." They do not recognize how rare the capacity to enjoy such liberties has been for the human race, and on how profound a philosophical and moral base the system of liberty depends.

Solzhenitsyn diagnoses correctly the kind of silly optimism

about the liberated individual that characterizes our culture. The word "evil" is not one that enlightened persons like to use. Excess, mistake, environmental influences, error of judgment, temporary loss of sanity—these categories feel comfortable. To attribute evil, or malice, or the demonic to human will seems to draw upon old-fashioned religious categories that are too harsh and unforgiving.

It is fascinating, indeed, to note that our nationally syndicated columnists, cultural leaders, and editorialists frequently castigate the American public in terms harsher than those used by Solzhenitsyn. They call our people too rich, soft, flabby, greedy, selfish, gluttonous, decadent, self-preoccupied, narrow, racist, imperialist, militarist, corrupt. Eugene Ionesco recently described in *Le Figaro* what he discovered in America:

Americans want to feel guilty. They have this need to be guilty. It is a masochism that we have already seen in France not so long ago. I found myself wanting to cheer them up, these Americans. I tried to do just that. . . . For the liberal anti-Americans, nothing good can come of the United States, even now. You have to call them Nazis, racists, and insist that their consumer society is worse than any of the underdeveloped societies. Call them names, insult them, that's their medicine [reprinted in the *Miami Herald*, January 7, 1979].

Solzhenitsyn diagnoses the sources of this feeling: "This tilt of freedom toward evil has come about gradually. It is founded on the humanistic and benevolent concept that man—the master of this universe—has no evil inherent in his nature; all the defects of life are caused by wrong social systems that must be corrected."

In a strange way, departments of sociology and psychology all over America seem to teach, as do the newspapers, that the individual has no moral weight of his or her own but that all good or evil comes from the social system. Individual morality is only a matter of therapy, as through such books as *Looking Out for Number One, Self-Assertiveness Training,* and *I'm OK, You're OK*. All moral questions become politicized. They have to do with being "liberated" from structures. Here, indeed, is the secret link of current liberal collectivism in the West with Marxist collectivism, about which Solzhenitsyn speaks so eloquently. Again Ionesco:

> Of 100 American students, 95 are apolitical and five are Marxists; but the latter are active, more effective. Those who go by the title of American intellectual—that is, journalists, novelists, actors, publishers, lawyers—are liberal, despite all the historical errors imputable to liberalism in the past fifty years. This state of mind exists in New York as well as Los Angeles. "God is dead, Marx is dead, and I don't feel too good either," as one of the street slogans put it during the 1968 student demonstrations in France [*Le Figaro;* reprinted in the *Miami Herald,* January 7, 1979].

Solzhenitsyn grasps with perfect clarity the secret bond between liberal humanism and Marxism. Citing Marx's assertion in 1844 that "communism is naturalized humanism," he comments:

> This proved to be not entirely without reason. There are common stones in the foundation of a humanism that has been eroded and any of the varieties of socialism: boundless materialism, freedom from religion and from religious responsibility (under communism driven as far as antireligious dictatorship), and concentration on social structures trying to be scientific (the Enlightenment of the eighteenth century and Marxism). It is not a coincidence that all communist rhetoric concerns Man (with a capital *M*) and his earthly happiness. A rather ugly comparison, isn't it—common traits in the perception of the world and the way of life in today's East and West! But such is the logic of materialism's development.
>
> Moreover, in the interrelationship of this kinship, the law is such that the brand of materialism that is further to the left and therefore more consistent always proves to be stronger, more attractive, and victorious. . . . During the past centuries, and especially in recent decades, as the process became more acute, the alignment of the world powers was as follows: liberalism was inevitably pushed aside by radicalism, radicalism had to surrender to socialism, and socialism could not stand up to communism. The communist regime in the East could endure and grow precisely because of enthusiastic sup-

port from an enormous number of Western intellectuals, who (feeling the kinship!) refused to see communism's crimes. When they could no longer ignore them, they tried to justify them. So it is: in the East, communism has suffered a total ideological defeat. It declined to zero. And yet Western intellectuals still look at it with considerable interest and sympathy.

Those who speak with the most moral conviction, the most certainty, the most fervor in America today are those who are vaguely Marxist. Ionesco notes it. Solzhenitsyn notes it. The editorials of the *New York Times,* even while seeming to be anti-Marxist, while pretending to a humble tolerance, a cautious pragmatism, a liberal diffidence, do not often prevail against the harsh moral claims of those farther to the left. In the face of certainty, what can they do who, in principle, must deprive themselves of a contrary certainty?

It is true that religion in America—Protestant, Catholic, and Jewish—has been uncommonly unintellectual, narrow, and dogmatic. Perhaps in unconscious opposition, the enlightened have prided themselves on "not pretending to have the answers," on being tolerant and pragmatic, on not arguing about moral principles or absolutes. A pluralistic society had to learn early that men and women of diverse backgrounds, moral convictions, and religious commitments need not come to explicit agreement on fundamental principles but could move forward by agreeing on practical courses of action. "Practical humanism," Jacques Maritain called this; "ecumenism," "pluralistic unity," "a common faith," others have called it.

But the deficiency in this arrangement is now becoming painfully apparent, four generations after the great immigrations that thickened the nation's pluralism (making this effectively a Catholic and Jewish as well as a Protestant nation, and incidentally creating room for public non-believers). As long as diverse traditions are studied, nourished, and kept publicly effective, their divergence freshens the streams of faith and commitment that water our democratic institutions. But as the young of each successive generation learn less and less about their roots, and become (in principle) more tolerant and (in practice) more indifferent to the spiritual inheritance of which they are the carriers, the pluralistic arrangement degenerates into "do your own thing." Anything.

The "me decade" did not result from a sudden effusion of selfishness or decadence; it is the logical consequence of a public surface tolerance combined with a loss of individual historical depth. In a sense, people become more like one another (wear the same clothes, go to the same schools, read the same books, are informed by the same media, go to the same parties, are "liberated" into the same mores). In another sense, they lose the social inheritances that, while differentiating them from one another, also instilled in them profound common values. Inwardly, each is animated by nothing more profound than personal preference and idiosyncrasy. Homogenized yet fragmented, the society of the supreme "me" (find yourself, be true to yourself) is the logical expression of a materialistic humanism.

Against this trend, of course, are spiritual revivals of many sorts as well as the continuing strength of many inherited moral principles that are still upheld by countless families and individuals, by some writers and artists, and in many churches, schools, and intellectual centers. A free society necessarily exhibits contradictory patterns of development, crosscurrents, and a paradoxical mix of weaknesses and strengths. Solzhenitsyn, after all, is *here;* he was invited to Harvard; many receive his words like water in the desert; many have waited and prepared themselves for an ultimate call to the deadly impending struggle.

The positive antipathy to religion common among the enlightened remains, however, a fundamental weakness in our culture. If there is no God, no natural order, no right and no wrong founded in the very nature of things, then human beings are free to make of the world what they will. Those who have confidence in the goodness of the individual heart have not yet encountered the Beast. They do not know what organized evil is. They cannot defend themselves against it. For far too long a time they try to "understand" it, to extend to it the sympathy they desire for themselves, to tolerate it, to make excuses for it, to evade its challenge. Then, after a time, beginning to see (or, more exactly, to feel, in their dreams and hidden fantasies) its strength, they become afraid, even paralyzed. Now they cannot move against it. First, they cannot easily admit how deeply they have been mistaken. Second, they lose heart at the prospect of how great a price they will have to pay to resist what has now become so strong. Some, fascinated by the sheer power of evil, join it. Others try to appease it.

This process has gone farther among us than we dare to admit. Our movies and television shows—the public record of our dreams—are filled today with images of disaster, flaming ruin, and devastation we dare not admit into public consciousness. We know well enough where we are headed. Paralysis grips us all.

Here religion ought to be a help, an awakener. But American religion has long relied upon a single chord: guilt. Accordingly, it strengthens in the public consciousness the very weaknesses Ionesco and Solzhenitsyn describe. In addition, American religion has been essentially privatistic. No theologian has yet created a theory of democratic capitalism, a religious theory that explains the basic institutions of the system that, at the cost of much historical struggling, finally appeared in human history, has had such spectacular and unprecedented moral and human successes, and now appears prematurely to be entering twilight.

Our preachers avoid institutional analysis. Those who take it up, evading the actual *history* of Marxism in the world these last sixty years, adopt a vulgar Marxist analysis. It is the organized churches that avert their eyes from the organized forces of repression in the imperial Soviet and analyze the world in terms of the private guilt of individual affluent Americans *vis-à-vis* the Third World, and that borrow Marxist propaganda to create a weapon of guilt for flaying their uncertain and predisposed followers. It is the churches that preach disarmament, urge tolerance for the Gulag Archipelago (not directly, of course, but in effect), support the forces of organized authoritarianism if only they will call themselves "liberation forces," and spread the doctrines of appeasement under the cloak of Christian charity. I invite Solzhenitsyn to inspect with care the pronouncements and policies of the World Council of Churches, the spiritual state and political perception of the leaders of "radical" and "liberal" religion (and even the sterility of "conservative" religion), the articles and editorials in our religious journals of opinion, and the utterances and deeds of our topmost political leaders who declare themselves publicly to be religious men—to inspect all this before he concludes that disaster will be averted through the agency of organized religion in the United States.

I can already hear his response. Perhaps, though, one must approach his final point by another route. Arthur J. Schlesinger, Jr., who claims to have learned much from Reinhold Niebuhr in politics, less so in religion, in his reply to Solzhenitsyn worried about "mysticism," and other secular critics called Solzhenitsyn an "enthusiast" or a "theocrat." But it is as much a matter of plain common sense, of down-to-earth reality, and even of cool pragmatism to speak of religion as not. It is true that Solzhenitsyn does not define the ideal institutional forms that would constitute his own conception of the good society. When he criticizes the society of the West and the society of the East—that "world split apart"—it is not clear what alternative he would propose. But his last few lines direct our gaze:

> If the world is not going to perish, it has at least reached a historic turning point, equal in importance to the turn from the Middle Ages to the Renaissance. This turn will demand a spiritual renewal from us so that we can ascend to a new, higher vision, to a new level of life, where our physical nature will not be condemned as in the Middle Ages—but, even more important, our spiritual nature will not be trampled upon as in modern times.
>
> This ascent is similar to climbing to the next anthropological stage. No one on earth has any other way left but—upward.

Two thinkers who move in the same world of vision as Solzhenitsyn and who have developed an intellectual model for a Christian humanism and a Christian culture are T. S. Eliot (see *Christianity and Culture,* Harcourt Brace, 1960) and Jacques Maritain (*Integral Humanism,* Notre Dame, 1973). Solzhenitsyn may at some point want to examine their work in order to differentiate from it his own vision. But I think we may use his own text to sketch a vision of a society worth building, a society whose heart is not so empty as that of our present civilization, a society that, while remaining pluralistic, is not relativistic. Every idea is not equal to every other, nor is every moral value equal to every other. There are actions that are good and actions that are evil. Dishonesty is not equal to honesty, nor cowardice to courage, nor apathy to compassion, nor degradation to dignity, nor slavery to liberty. A society that, in order to defend diversity and tolerance, permits everything equally will suffer the same fate as an individual who refuses to make moral choices, who merely shrugs, "What's the difference?" Even without a resolute enemy, such a person, like such a society, would have doomed himself. And a resolute enemy will find him thoroughly defenseless.

Religion itself is subject to many historical permutations. Like liberty, it is a dangerous part of human life; one without the other destroys itself. Morever, religion has many forms: not only the various concrete traditions of Christianity and Judaism that have shaped the West, but also those several forms of classical "natural" religion, like stoicism and various forms of unclosed humanism, that have helped to form the legal and intellectual foundations of the West. The life of the spirit to which Solzhenitsyn calls us need not be sectarian, narrow, or lacking in ecumenical awareness. Indeed, he has taken pains to speak of it in words that belong to no one tradition alone, avoiding even the intimate symbols of his own beloved Russian Orthodoxy. He has raised the discussion to a pluralistic plane on which those of varying commitments may join.

A liberal, pluralistic, constitutional democracy would not in the least be falsified, moreover, by being rooted in institutions sharply defined by the vision of man that Solzhenitsyn sketches: imperfect, untrustworthy, requiring every sort of institutional check and balance. The Bill of Rights would not violate the civilization to which he beckons us. In such a civilization he surely would insist upon freedom of the press—but a press that operates fairly and responsibly. His complaint about the Western press is that its freedom has been paralyzed by the tyranny of fashion and the absence of a genuine competition of ideas. One who finds no substantial intellectual difference between the world of *Time* and the world of *Newsweek,* between the *Washington Post* and the *New York Times,* or between ABC, CBS, and NBC, would find it hard to object to his criticism of the present too-narrow reality. In a word, none of the institutions we so cherish in the West would be undone in the world Solzhenitsyn envisages.

But the spirit that inhabits them, infuses them, and directs them he most certainly asks us to change. From relativism and moral indifference (you follow your values, I'll follow mine), Solzhenitsyn calls us to moral choice and moral self-criticism, to *growth* in the values we claim to hold. His assumption here, if I follow him, is sound: on the surface, one value system (Christianity) seems to differ from another (Judaism), but at the depths the most serious seekers after truth come to unexpected and remarkable convergences.

The world split apart has at its center a powerful longing to draw all together. Solzhenitsyn's vision is not antithetical to the political institutions conceived, in part, under the aegis of the Enlightenment and anthropocentric humanism. But it does implant these institutions in their inmost center.

Ethics and Public Policy Reprints

Reprints are $1 each. Postpaid if payment accompanies order.
Orders of $10 or more, 10 per cent discount.